MARCHING ORDERS

D0494213

MARCHING ORDERS

Daily Readings for Younger People

by

WILLIAM BARCLAY

edited and introduced
by Denis Duncan

EVESHAM

Published by
ARTHUR JAMES LIMITED
THE DRIFT EVESHAM WORCS.
ENGLAND

Compilation copyright © 1973 by Denis Duncan

First published in Great Britain 1973 by Hodder & Stoughton Ltd.

with

The Saint Andrew Press

PUBLISHED IN THIS EDITION BY
ARTHUR JAMES, EVESHAM, WORCS., ENGLAND

British Library C.I.P.

Barclay, William, *1907–1978*
  Marching orders: daily readings for younger
  people.
  1. Youth—Religious life   2. Christian life
  I. Title   II. Duncan, Denis
  242′.2   BV4531.2

  ISBN 0–85305–251–4

Printed and bound in Great Britain by
Cox & Wyman Ltd, Reading

CONTENTS

MEET WILLIAM BARCLAY

Take a brilliant brain, a photographic mind, a friendly nature, a conductor's baton, some railway engines, a football, and a Christian character, put them all together and hey, presto, you have someone like Dr. William Barclay!

Dr. Barclay is one of the most famous and popular Christian writers of all times. Millions of his books have been sold, translated into foreign languages, travelled the world.

Millions of people have seen him on TV or heard him on radio.

Many of your fathers and mothers have known and loved this extraordinary man.

So we thought you would like to know him too.

You will find he says so many important things, so many profound things, so many relevant things. You will find he touches real depths and yet he can be so amusing, and so "child-like". You will find him so human—he had his own family, his own dog and cat, and his own model train-set, etc.

In this book, I have taken Dr. Barclay's writings for older people and re-written them (with his permission!) for you. Your parents will recognise this material and where it comes from (especially from my own *Through the Year with William Barclay*, published by Hodder and Stoughton in 1971). But in its form here, it will be quite new to you.

I hope you will enjoy meeting this great, great man, and profit from his thoughts and his faith.

I am sure you will!

DENIS DUNCAN

William Barclay died in 1978 but his words and his thoughts live on.

DD

MONTH ONE

Do you lose things?
Lost Property Offices are filled with all kinds of things you would never expect people to lose!

But there are some things in life you should never lose.

You should never lose *your temper*.
You should never lose *your head*.
You should never lose *hope*.

Your temper

Anyone who flies off into a temper really has a problem in life. If you lose your temper, you will do things for which you will later be very sorry.

When anyone wanted to enter the famous Qumran Community from which the Dead Sea Scrolls came, he was asked how he got on with people. The thing that mattered for living in the community was the ability to get on with others. Temper was no use there.
Don't lose yours!

Your head

> If you can keep your head when all about you
> Are losing theirs and blaming it on you

then you will find true manhood, said Rudyard Kipling.

In times of danger, to keep your head is a great asset.
Don't lose yours!

Your hope

Most artists have painted Hope as young and eager, with head thrown back and face laughing to the wind. But Watts knew better. He painted Hope as battered and bleeding and tattered, with only one string left on her lyre. But with her eyes alight.

Christians have hope always.
We are saved by hope, said St. Paul (Rom. 8: 24).

Don't lose yours!

Read Romans 5: 3–5.

YOUR HOPES   Day Two

Have you heard this story about Alexander the Great?

Feeling very generous one day, he decided to give some of
his "possessions" away.
To one man he gave a fortune.
To another a whole province.
To yet another a very important position in his court.
"If you keep on doing that" said a friend, "you will have
nothing left."
"Don't you believe it" said Alexander. "I've kept the most
valuable thing of all to myself—my hopes for the future!"

If you really want to find happiness in life, have plenty of
hopes!

Read 1 Thessalonians 5: 4–8.

KEEP HOPING!   Day Three

What are *your* hopes for the future?
A good job?
Plenty of friends?
Lots of travel?
Meeting interesting people?

It doesn't matter what they are—so long as they are
worthwhile.
The main thing is *keep hoping*!

Older people have found life begins to lose its point when
they are no longer able to live in hope.

You are young.
With so much to hope for.

Like Alexander, hold on to your hopes!
They will keep you going forward.

Read Hebrews 11: 1–3.

HAPPINESS Day Four

Here are two more ways to find real happiness!
But you may be surprised at the first.
It is work!

None of us likes the thought of work much. "I'm going
to do nothing for ever and ever," says an old poem. Doesn't
it sound attractive?
But you ask people who have been unemployed for a long
time how *they* feel about it. They would give anything for
something to do.

To have something worthwhile to do really does help us
to be happy.

The other way to happiness is to have someone to love.
It may be much later in life before you realise the truth
of that.
But it *is* true.
Happiness involves loving—and being loved!

It also means loving God.
And knowing he loves you.

Read Psalm 146: 1–5.

TIME FLIES! Day Five

Time flies!
Or as the Romans put it: *tempus fugit.*
Use it!

Here are some odd facts!
Breakfast time takes ten minutes (I guess!)
Lunch time takes twenty minutes.
Teatime takes another twenty minutes.
Supper adds ten minutes more.
In other words, you spend one hour in a normal day just *eating*.
Or seven hours a week.
So we spend about fifteen days a year just eating!
If you live to be seventy, you will have spent *three years* just eating.

What about sleeping?
Eight hours a night—on average (it's more at your age but it gets less, hence the average) i.e., a third of each full day of twenty-four hours. Or in seventy years life, about twenty-four years asleep!
No wonder *tempus fugit*! So much of it is just eating and sleeping!
We must use our non-eating, non-sleeping time well.
How?
Learning! About life and the one without whom life is meaningless—God.

Read 1 Samuel 3: 1–10.

NOW IS THE TIME!

Let's look more closely at the time we spend learning.

There are 365 days in a year.
But with no school on Saturday or Sunday, we have to deduct 104 days, leaving 261.
Then there are holidays. These vary in different parts of the country, but if we take fourteen off for Christmas, fourteen at Easter plus say sixty more for summer, half terms, etc. we get eighty-eight more days to deduct, making 173.
We do not however go to school *all* day, only for about

14

six hours—or a quarter of a day. So about forty-three days in the year is our school time actually!

One third we spend sleeping.
One ninth we spend at school.
So we spend nearly three times as long sleeping as learning!

"*Now* is the time" says the Bible.
The time to learn about life, the world and God is really quite short.
So use it all.
Fully.

Read Galatians 4: 1–11.

A PARERGON

Be sure you have a parergon!
You agree? More likely you are wondering what on earth a parergon is!

I'll tell you.

I once met a man who was a professor of Applied Mathematics. But he also wrote a commentary on I Corinthians!
It is that extra thing they do that is their parergon.

I know many people who have parergons.
For example:
A professor of Italian who is also a bird-watcher.
A professor of Aeronautics who is an actor.
A professor of Naval Architecture who is an organist.
A professor of Dentistry who writes children's stories.
A professor of Maths. who is an expert in Gaelic.
A professor of Mechanical Engineering who is a poet.
An astronomer who writes thrillers.

To do two things at once in this case is good. Our job should not take all our time and attention. The parergons people have added have often been great contributions to life.

Have *you* a parergon?
It may well be a blessing to you.
And to others.
And to God.
For many people have found it is in their parergons— their extra things—they have done most for God.

Read 1 Corinthians 10: 23–31.

CONCENTRATE! Day Eight

Do you find it hard to concentrate?
I do!
But there are two things that have helped me to concentrate better.
The first is having a real *interest* in what I'm doing.
The second is *a long-term view* on what I'm doing.

Piano practice is a bore. But when it is seen as a "long-term" necessity, it begins to be bearable.
Athletic training can be very dull, but when the thought of taking part in the Olympic Games, or even in some lesser competition, is present, it is a little easier to carry on!

Concentration in all things is necessary. Even in your growth in the Christian life.

That is why it tells us in Hebrews to "look unto Jesus".
Concentration on *him* works wonders!

Read Hebrews 12: 1–2.

CHANGE YOUR MIND! Day Nine

Do you assume that *you* are always right?
If so, you will never be a good scholar or student.

Learning means accepting the fact that your view may be wrong, that to change your view is not a sign of weakness but of character.

This is very true in trying to understand the Bible.

The *Nestlé* editions of the New Testament (which have long been valued for their help and wisdom) have this quotation by a famous commentator called Bengel, printed at the top of the preface page: "Apply yourself wholly to the text, then apply the whole to yourself."

To learn from the Bible, we must not simply regard our study as a "mental hike" (as somebody has called it). When we study the Bible we are looking for an answer to the question asked by the prophet: "Lord what will you have *me* to do?"

It is not *our* interpretation of that answer we seek, but what God is really saying through his word.

To get that answer may well change our minds about what is right for us!

As it did for St. Paul!

Read Acts 22: 1–21.

MY BROTHER'S KEEPER? Day Ten

Cain, in the book of Genesis, asked a strange question when he was quizzed by God about the death of Abel. "Am I my brother's keeper?" he said.

We are our brother's keeper in that we are responsible for the welfare of other people. We should care if others get hurt or are drawn into doing wrong.

"Silence is golden", people say.

But it isn't really so good if it means saying nothing about wrongs others are suffering. What happens to poor people, old people, coloured people, ill people *is* our responsibility, and we must accept it.

To be your brother's keeper may mean you must *speak up*!

Read Genesis 4: 1–13.

THE OPTIMIST AND THE PESSIMIST   Day Eleven

Are you an optimist?
Or a pessimist?

"It is a good thing to have an optimist at the front provided there is a pessimist at the rear."
So said the famous British Prime Minister, Lord Asquith.
In other words, in a big undertaking both attitudes are useful!

The optimist is the kind of man who sees possibilities in everything. He will always try to find a solution to the problem. "It can be done somehow," he will say. "Everything will be all right in the end."
The man who will "have a bash at it" is a useful man.

The pessimist is cautious. He wants to see the way clearly. He is slow to commit himself. He is afraid a difficult undertaking may end in failure.
There is value in that man too.

The Greeks liked to divide men into two kinds—those who needed the spur and those who needed the rein.
Jesus had both kinds among the disciples!
There was Peter and there was Thomas. But *both* played a part with Jesus, in his mission.

The leader saw to that!

Read St. Luke 5: 1–11; St. John 20: 24–29.

18

I have been reading an interesting book. It is the life of Sir Halley Stewart, churchman and industrialist, founder of the Sir Halley Stewart Trust, who was born in 1838 and died in his hundredth year in 1937.

This book showed the wide difference between the Victorian and the present age.

And what differences!

Take the *family* situation.

Halley Stewart's father, Alexander Stewart, was one of twelve children; he married a girl who was one of a family of seven daughters; he himself had fourteen children, of whom Halley was the tenth. To use an Irishism—if Halley Stewart had been alive today, the chances are he would never have been born at all! Here we have three marriages with a product of thirty-three children—common enough a hundred years ago, most unlikely today.

Take *Sundays*.

Alexander Stewart ran a school. Here is the time-table for the ordinary Sunday: seven a.m. prayer meeting for the scholars and the family; eight a.m. breakfast; nine a.m. School Scripture class; nine thirty a.m. Sunday School; eleven a.m. church service; one p.m. dinner; two thirty p.m. Sunday School followed by a walk; five p.m. tea; six thirty p.m. church service; eight p.m. singing in the home.

That was a Sunday in a pious home a hundred years ago. Today it would be incredible.

Take the *servants*.

Halley Stewart did not run a very big house; but there is a photograph of the house staff taken in about 1896. There are three gardeners, a coachman, a cowman, cook, scullery maid, parlourmaid, housemaid, washerwoman and two other assistants who were gardeners' wives.

What a vast difference there is as time passes.
Yet one thing remains the same.
Our need of help spiritually.

The answer to that need?
"Jesus Christ, the same yesterday, today and for ever."
In Victorian, Elizabethan, stone or space age, that truth
is *always* the same.

Read Hebrews 13: 1–8.

"SWOPPETS" Day Thirteen

Have you ever heard of "swoppets"?
They are little toy figures—often cowboys and Indians on
horseback. But the point about them is that you can take
the head off one figure and put it on another. Or you can take
the rider off one horse and put him on another.
These "swoppets" can give great fun!

It would be fun too if we could do that with human
beings! Then you might get some very valuable combina-
tions.
For example:
A is determined: B is gentle.
C is good but cold: D is reckless but warm.
If we could put the best of these combinations together,
we would have some marvellous people.

People aren't "swoppets", of course, so we cannot change
them about in this way.
But they can be changed quite a bit.
Jesus, says the Bible, can make "new men'.' And this is
what our Christian faith is about.
It "makes all things new".

Read Ephesians 4: 17–24.

Do you like reading?

I am sure you do, because it is *the* way to learn and to enjoy—at the same time.

The great writer, Robert Southey, is said to have been quite miserable if he wasn't half-way through a book!

John Wesley, one of the greatest evangelists of all time and founder of the Methodist Church, insisted that his helpers read.

"Steadily spend all morning in this employ," he writes, "or at least five hours in the twenty-four."

(Incidentally, though he was constantly travelling and preaching, he played a part in over 350 publications, either writing them himself, or with his brother, Charles).

If anyone said to John: "But I have no taste for reading," he would reply: "Then contract a taste for it, or return to your trade."

He underlined this over and over again. "Reading Christians will be knowing Christians," he said. "The work of grace will die in one generation if the Methodists are not a reading people."

If you want to *know*, read.

If you want to know the faith, read too.
Not least, the Bible.

Read Nehemiah 8: 1–8.

WRITE!   **Day Fifteen**

Do you hate having to write letters?
Perhaps you do.
But letter-writing is important in life.

"Dear Letter, go on your way o'er mountain, plain or sea;
God bless all who speed your flight to where I wish you to
    be
And bless all those beneath the roof
where I would bid you rest;
But bless even more the one to whom this letter is ad-
    dressed."

This is not good poetry or verse, but it says something
that is true.

Letters help friendships along. "A man should keep his
friendships in good repair," said the famous Dr. Johnson.

So letters can—
say thanks;
express sympathy;
help to keep memory alive;
encourage;
share exciting news.

St. Paul did all this in his letters—preserved for ever in
our New Testament.

A postage stamp has power!
Write!

Read Galatians 6: 6–11.

LETTERS AGAIN! Day Sixteen

Here are some rules for letter-writers.

Write now!
So often we put off that note we should send. So often
that is a pity.

For if a letter is going to be sent, it should almost certainly
be sent *at once or not at all!*

Write clearly!

I once sent a letter to Fife. It ended up in Fiji!

There is no need to ask why!

So let it be a matter of courtesy to write clearly. A letter is meant to be read.

It should be readable!

"You are a letter from Christ," said St. Paul to the Corinthian Christians.

Through *you*, Jesus is made known.

To send a letter is good.

To *be* one is even better!

Read 2 Corinthians 3: 1–3.

RULING PASSIONS   Day Seventeen

One of the greatest football matches ever played took place at the famous Hampden Park Stadium in Glasgow. It was the European Cup Final—Real Madrid *v.* Eintracht.

There were many famous players in these Spanish and German teams, but none more famous than Puskas, the Hungarian genius who played for Real.

On the morning after the Final, Puskas was interviewed by the Press. Among the things he said was this: "When I don't *play* football, I *talk* football. When I don't talk football, I *think* football."

There are many ruling passions that grip men.

The golfer will spend hour after hour almost fanatically trying to get some part of his game just right. The cricketer will walk around with a ball in his hand, even as he goes about his business, strengthening his fingers by gripping.

The gambler can have such a passion for gambling that he will denude his house of all his possessions and starve his family to get money to stake.

The alcoholic will come to a stage when he cannot exist without his liquor.

The man who is out for money will spend all day trying to find ways of making and saving it, and his nights in dreaming of it.

There are some wrong ruling passions there, aren't there? It is important to get the right one.

Paul said his ruling passion was Christ.
"For me to live *is* Christ," he said:

It makes you think, doesn't it, about your ruling passion?

Read Philippians 1: 12–21.

SAINTS

How would you define a saint?
Here are some definitions that have been given.

"A saint is someone who makes it easier to believe in God."

"A saint is someone in whom Christ lives again."

"A saint is someone the light shines through."

I like that last definition.
So did a little boy who could not understand what a saint was until, one day, the sun shone right through a figure in the stained glass window of the church he attended. Then it clicked! A saint *is* someone the light shines through.

Jesus said this too in the Sermon on the Mount, when he talked about discipleship.
"Let your light shine before men" he said, so that people through you see all that is good.
Yes, perhaps a saint is best described in that third definition.
Someone the light shines through.

Read St. John 13: 31–35.

THE RIGHT BALANCE Day Nineteen

There are things that matter, and things that don't matter. The secret of a happy life is to get the right balance between the important and the unimportant.

Lloyd George, the famous British Prime Minister, once invited Ramsay Macdonald, also a Prime Minister during his political career, to discuss some important issues—especially unemployment.
"Did you make any progress?" Lloyd George was asked.
The fiery Welshman blazed with indignation.
"Progress?" he said. "He insisted on discussing the old Dutch masters!"

The famous painters we call the Dutch masters *are* important, but weren't in that particular conversation about urgent political matters!
It is all a matter of balance and proportion.

"Seek first the Kingdom," said Jesus, and the other things will be all right.
In other words, get your priorities right!

This we must all do—to "find" life.

Read Mark 3: 31–35.

GIFTS Day Twenty

One of the happiest men I ever knew was a man who worked in a garage in my home town.
Oh no, he wasn't a highly skilled mechanic!
He just washed dirty cars!

What pride he took in that work!
You could run your hand under the wing of the car, and it was spotless!
He was marvellous!

25

What the world needs (someone has said) are not so much people who can do extraordinary things. It needs people who can do ordinary things extraordinarily well.

A bus conductress can take your fare in a way that lights up the whole day.

A shop assistant can serve you in a way that makes the world a better place.

We all have gifts, ordinary as they may seem.
It is for us to use these gifts, to bless the world.
And in doing that, we will be (as the Bible says) "glorifying God."

Read I Corinthians 12: 27–31a.

INFECTION   Day Twenty-one

Through the wonders of modern medicine, we can be inoculated against infections of many kinds.

If you are travelling to the Far East, you must be protected against diseases common in that area. So you are inoculated against them.

There are infections of other kinds in life. We have to be careful about these too.

For example there is the bad influence of "porn"—pornography that is—the flood of literature that only wants to stimulate us in a wrong way.

We can not be "isolated" (to use another medical word) in life. We have to live in the world where there is a lot of temptation to do wrong. We need all the help—and helps—we can get to encourage us to seek the things which are "good and lovely and of good report" (Phil. 4: 8).

The biggest help of all is of course Jesus himself.
His example and his influence are truly an inoculation against infection in our *spiritual* lives.

Read St. John 6: 35–48.

Some of you will be natural leaders. Others won't have this gift. But more of you will increase your capacity for leadership if you understand the essentials of it.

King George VI had an impediment in his speech. It was not a stutter. It was really what we call a "stop".

One day he was seeing over a film studio. By what seemed an unfortunate coincidence, the engineer who was showing him round had exactly the same impediment. In his nervousness the engineer found it becoming worse and worse.

King George put his hand on the man's shoulder. "It's all right, friend," he said. "I know what it's like."

Here was true understanding.

During the Second World War that king's brother, the Duke of Kent, was killed in a plane crash. The King's own home, Buckingham Palace, was bombed. He knew what war meant too. He was personally involved.

When the leaders are *involved*, the supporters find it easier to follow.

Read St. Matthew 24: 1–14.

THE TRUE LEADER   **Day Twenty-three**

One of the secrets of Field Marshal Montgomery's leadership was that he was known by sight.

He did not sit, hidden, at his H.Q.

He went out and met and knew his men.

The man who leads is the man who is known.

Half the battle in any cause is discovering *what* is wrong and what needs to be done.

When you pass your driving test, it would be useful also to know what happens under the bonnet. When cars break down, the mechanic comes and often, with a quick look, diagnoses the trouble. We could, on many occasions, have put it right ourselves and saved time and money if we had only known how to repair it.

A leader must have the insight to see and to know what should be done.
And help his supporters to do it.

Read St. Matthew 16: 21–28.

THE TIME TO ACT   Day Twenty-four

Jeeves, the famous butler in P. G. Wodehouse's stories, used to say: "There is always a way."
A man called Cavour said that the first essential of successful action is the sense of the impossible.

Far too often we look at bad situations and decide nothing can be done.
'There is always a way.'

A leader must have the resources to decide what must be done for success to be attained.

"For the right moment, you must wait: when the time comes, you must strike hard."
So said Quinctus Fabius Cunctator, a Roman leader.

A leader must know the moment to act and know how to act in that moment.
"There is always a way."

Read Nehemiah 2: 1–8.

GOOD OR BAD   Day Twenty-five

On the retreat from Dunkirk in the Second World War, despite apparent defeat, the Guards held a kit inspection, landed in England and marched off as if on a ceremonial parade!

Tradition can mean a great deal.

Even today, a bride is on a bridegroom's left arm in order to leave his right arm—the sword arm—free to meet a crisis!

Even today, when a man walks on the outside of a lady on the pavement it is because, before roads were surfaced, he walked there to shield her from the mud thrown up by horses' hooves and carriage wheels!

Tradition can be good and bad.
If it adds something useful or fine, it is good.
If it sets up barriers ("we never did it *that* way here!"), it is bad.

Encourage traditions that are good.
They will add to life.
Jesus did this.

Discourage traditions that are bad.
They cause fossilising!
Jesus would have none of that!

Read Haggai 2: 1–9.

I REMEMBER, I REMEMBER . . .   Day Twenty-six

I remember the time when an aeroplane was an incredible sight.

I remember when motor cars were rarities.

I remember the first wireless sets.

I remember the first ball-point pens—how rare they were and how expensive!

I remember when you could buy cigarettes for 4p for twenty and petrol at 7p a gallon.

Do you think I would put the clock back if I could?
No, I wouldn't.
For there are other things I remember.

I remember when there was no National Health Service.

I remember when people could not have proper medical attention because they could not pay for it.

I remember when my work, week after week, included visits to patients in sanatoriums, for tuberculosis was a scourge then!

I remember children with rickets and diphtheria.

Do you think I would like to go back to that?

I remember when only the very wealthy had a car; when to eat in a restaurant was unusual for ordinary people; when a holiday in Spain would have seemed a dream; when many people had no holidays at all.

I don't want to go back to a situation like that at all.

"Thank God things can never be the same again" said the great Scottish preacher, A. J. Gossip, surprisingly. But rightly.

It cannot be God's will that the things of life should be so unevenly shared or that pain should be borne unnecessarily.

To change what needs to be changed is what God would have his caring people do.

Read Timothy 1: 12–16.

ONE FARTHING — Day Twenty-seven

St. John's-Renfield Church in Glasgow celebrated its one hundred and fiftieth anniversary in 1969. A brochure, with a brief but vivid history of the congregation, was issued to mark the event.

Among the many interesting things in that account is the story of the opening of Free St. John's Church in George Street on June 8, 1845. The collection that day was made up as follows:

Banknotes: 2 at £100, 22 at £20, 7 at £10, 95 at £5, 444 at £1.

Gold: 1 old guinea, 10 sovereigns, 23 half-sovereigns.

Silver: 52 crowns, 1 American dollar, 420 half-crowns, 627 shillings, 393 sixpences, 53 fourpences, 2 threepences, 1 twopence.

Copper: 48 pennies, 42 half-pennies, and 1 farthing.

To this had to be added £12. 3s. 4d. in the evening collection and £8 2s. 9d. of donations from people who were absent—a grand total of £1,779 17s. 10d.—and one farthing.

This farthing fascinates me.
Who gave it and why did he give it?

There are three possibilities.

Perhaps a very mean person put into the collection: the smallest sum he could find.

Perhaps it was all some poor person had to give—a widow's mite, in fact.

Perhaps somebody turned out his pockets and gave all he had—even to the last farthing.

If it was the first possibility, it is best forgotten.
If it was the second, a good deed was done and one which God would honour.
If it was the third, then God would be pleased again.
Blessed (and therefore happy) is the man who gives all for his faith.

In which category would *you* be?

Read St. Luke 21: 1–4.

A MAGNIFYING GLASS   Day Twenty-eight

You are all familiar with magnifying glasses. But have you ever thought of your mind as a magnifying glass?
It can be!

Do you sometimes *magnify* what you do? Some people behave as if they were carrying the whole world on *their* shoulders. Some young people do this too. But it isn't a very useful occupation. It's much better getting down to what needs to be done rather than talking about how much there is to do!

Do you ever *magnify* the harder aspects of life? Some people do. They have (as we say), "a chip on their shoulders" about life. "Why does everything go wrong for *me*?" they ask.

St. Paul has a useful comment on this. He reminds the Corinthians that whatever happens to us has happened to others at one time or another. To think *we* are badly treated by God is a poor way to look at life.

So like what you do.
See it as a vocation from God.
If you do that, you won't have time to spend worrying about how badly *you* have been treated!

Read I Corinthians 4: 1–10.

THE BIBLE   Day Twenty-nine

What a wonderful book the Bible is!
It is always relevant. Always helpful.
For it is about life.

If you look into the Bible you will find perhaps to your surprise, that it has a lot to say (for example) to craftsmen.
The doctor finds his skills discussed in Leviticus.
The lawyer and the judge will feel at home in Deuteronomy.
The preacher can study the message of the teaching of the prophets.
The soldier and the military leader will find battles and campaigns to analyse.

The traveller ...
The ornithologist ...
The archaeologist ...
The geographer ...
The builder ... Why, the description of the detail of the Temple is a fascinating mine of information for any craftsman to wonder at!

The housewife will find herself in the parables of our Lord.

Is it not amazing that such an old book can be so topical and so relevant?

Read Leviticus 13: 24–28.

INSPIRED!   Day Thirty

The Bible has a flair for speaking to us whatever our need is.

It brings comfort in time of sorrowing.
It brings guidance in time of difficulty.
It brings challenge in time of hesitation.

You cannot in fact find any part of life about which the Bible does not speak.

The Bible is a guide and help in worship.
The Bible is a mine of information.
The Bible is the book of life.
In fact the Bible is God's book!

For only sheer inspiration could create such a wonderful book!

Read Isaiah 40: 18–28.

TRADITION   Day Thirty-one

At a conference in St. Andrews I met a very charming Nigerian called Agwu Oji, who was going to Nigeria to be a bishop of the united Church there. He was going back to his own land and his own people to be one of the chosen leaders of the Christian Church in West Africa.

After evening prayers one night Agwu Oji and I were leaving the chapel together and I suddenly had an idea. I said to him, "Before you go back to Nigeria, would you like to go and stand for once in the pulpit from which John Knox, the famous Scottish reformer, preached?" A Church of Scotland missionary, who has served for more than a quarter of a century in Nigeria was standing beside us. "Oji," he said, "is far too humble a man to go and do that by himself, unless you take him." So I took Oji by the arm and the two of us walked across the chapel and went up the steps and stood for a moment in that very pulpit from which John Knox had preached.

For me that was one of the great moments of that conference.

A tradition as we have already agreed can be a great influence on us, can't it? Just think of the great traditions there are in football teams, theatres, schools. When we think of those who have been there before us, we find it an inspiration.

Perhaps in your school you are inspired by your tradition.

What is even more important, you are helping to create one—now.

The other thing I liked about that occasion was the fact that black and white were together.

Which is as it should be.

You only get true harmony out of the piano if you use black keys and white.

It's true of life too.

Read Psalm 137: 1–5.

MONTH TWO

GOD LISTENS Day One

God listens to our prayers.
Is that hard to believe?
It is true.

No one is too small to pray to God, or too unimportant.
God listens ...
No one is too great.
God listens.

You can pray at any time. God never "slumbers or sleeps"
(says the Psalmist).
God listens ...

No one is too young to pray to God.
No one is too old.
To both, God listens.

And the wonder of God is that *he* listens to each one of us
as if we were the only ones in the world!

Read St. Matthew 6: 5–8.

PRAYER Day Two

Prayer has its own laws.
Here is one of them.

*Prayer is not God doing things for us. Prayer is God
helping us to do things for ourselves.*
It is a law of prayer that God will not do for us what we
can do for ourselves. God is not an "easy way out".

Sometimes you may bring an exercise home from school.
You ask your parents to help. But your parents know that,
though they could do the exercise for you, this isn't really a
help at all. The real help is to explain, to guide and to
encourage.

So when we pray, it's not really a case of unloading our problems and tasks on to God.

Prayer is the way by which God helps us to do successfully what we have to do.

Read St. Matthew 6: 9–15.

THE GOLDEN HANDLE   Day Three

We sometimes think that prayer is getting God to do things for us.

It really is God helping us to do things for ourselves.

Epictetus, the philosopher of olden times, said that everything in the world had two handles. One was made of lead and the other of gold.

How we tackle things depends on which handle we use!

The facts of any situation are constant. They don't change. It is how we approach the situation itself that matters. Whether we take the golden handle or the lead handle will determine how well we deal with it.

The value of our faith is that it gives us the courage to face the situation positively.

Or if you like, it leads us to the handle of gold.

"I can do all things through Christ who strengthens me."

Read Philippians 4: 8–13.

HELP ME TO HELP. . .   Day Four

Here is a prayer which a small boy wrote:
"Oh God, help us to be good and to help other people."

This is a very good prayer because:
    It says "*Help* us", not "*Make* us".
    It says "Help *us*", not "Help *me*".

It emphasises the good rather than the right. For good refers to value which is important.

It does not say "Help *others*". It says "Help *us* to help *others*". This is important, for this is the way God works.

It is not enough to pray for the aged and the lonely. We must visit them.

It is not enough to pray for missionary work abroad or at home. We must ask if *we* ought to be missionaries in every way we can.

Read James 2: 14–26.

THE ETERNAL TRIANGLE   Day Five

Sir Gilbert Scott, the great English architect, has an extraordinary claim to fame!

He designed Liverpool Cathedral *and* the telephone kiosk.

So—something of sheer grandeur and something of mere usefulness came from the mind and heart of the same man.

Dedication to your work can be expressed in little things as well as big things. To be "faithful in little things" is a real qualification for work.

But there is another fascinating truth from this story!

In a cathedral, men talk to God.

In a telephone kiosk, men talk to each other.

What more is there to say about man's link to God and his brother? You cannot (the Bible says) love God and hate your brother. Loving God implies loving your brother.

So a kiosk and a cathedral have a lot to say about "the eternal triangle" which is God, your brother and you!

Read 1 John 4: 20—5: 12

I am not very good at "jobs about the house", I am sorry to say. It is not that I am helpless. I just never have time!

So, sometimes, I am compelled to action—but it is at the wrong time and for the wrong reasons!

Like this, for example.

A painting job had to be done in our house, so a member of the family did it in a do-it-yourself way.

I did not think the job was done well!

I was therefore forced into action—after some well-chosen words of criticism—and did the job myself all over again! And, though I say it myself, I did do a very good job!

That, I see now, was the wrong way to do it.

It is always wrong to delay action until something goes wrong.

It is always wrong to be lazy enough to do nothing until something forces our hand.

Act now.
In time.
There is an urgency in life we should respect.
"*Now* is the accepted time. *Now* is the day of salvation."

Do it now!

Read Jeremiah 1: 4–10.

I told you yesterday about my experiment in house painting.

Well, the paint I was using was "non-drip".

This saves a lot of mess, but it does mean it is very thick. So there are right ways and wrong ways in using it.

That taught me something!

You must know *how* to do something to do it well.

40

Normally, in painting, you can sweep the brush backwards and forwards like a pendulum. But with *this* paint that was impossible.

If you drew the brush in one direction, you laid it on, but, if you swept the brush backwards in the reverse direction, off it came again!

So if you kept laying it on, but always in the same direction, you did a good job!

"Technique" is a word some people don't like. But whatever you are doing, be it painting a room, preaching a sermon, or playing a game, you get the best results if you "know how". Technique matters.

It is not a bad lesson about life either.
And there is a book that teaches know-how about living.
The Bible.
And of course a Person too.
Jesus.

Read St. John 10: 9–10.

AVOID TROUBLE! Day Eight

Have you heard of the great evangelist, D. L. Moody?

One day a man came to Moody with a very sorry story and asked: "Mr. Moody, what would *you* do if you got into a mess like that?"

"Man," said Moody, "I would never have got into it."

But of course he still helped him!

So many things need never have happened if only we had acted in time.

This is true too of international crises, industrial disputes, church quarrels, family upsets. If only someone had acted early on, the worst might never have happened.

So if, as you grow up, you see troubles starting between friends, or over the colour of a person's skin, see if *you* can act to prevent it from growing.

Reconciliation is a great Christian word. It may include, whatever else it means, helping to stop trouble before it starts.

To help people *in* trouble is right (as Moody showed). To help people *avoid* trouble is even better.

Read Romans 5: 6–11.

WHAT'S THE HURRY?   Day Nine

A man from the backwoods of Australia came to the great city of Sydney for the first time. His first question? "Why is everybody running?"

A certain gentleman visited the U.S.A. three times.

On the first visit, he thought all Americans thought about was *money*.

On the second visit, he thought most Americans were obsessed by *power*.

On the third, he decided the main aim in America was *speed*.

And that third impression remained (and it would be true of many more places than America).

"He who believes will not be in haste" said the prophet Isaiah (28: 16).

We would probably do a lot more, if we hurried less.

We would certainly do a lot more of a higher standard if we could learn to take our time.

Read Proverbs 3: 13–26.

SEE IT THROUGH   Day Ten

I learned from my decorating ploy that if you begin a

job, you must see it through. For if you stopped painting, then resumed again later, the "join" was all too easy to see.

How many things in life are only half done!
Most of us are better starters than finishers.
Think of some of the hobbies you have started—stamps, scrapbooks, and so on. We are very enthusiastic at the beginning but ...

"Blessed is he who endures to the end" it says in Matthew's Gospel.
See it through and you will get great satisfaction.

Read 2 Timothy 2: 8–14.

VICTORY   Day Eleven

The young man I had to examine had graduated as a Master of Arts with Honours in Mental Philosophy. It was as he entered his course of study for the ministry that I marked his Greek and English Bible papers.
He scored 94 per cent in the first and 86 per cent in the second.
He is totally blind.

How often seriously handicapped people have done great work and so won great victories.

Julius Caesar was an epileptic.
Augustus, the great Roman Emperor, had a stomach ulcer, so some historians believe.
Douglas Bader, that wartime flying ace, won his greatest triumphs after he lost his legs and had to use artificial ones.
This is victory!

If you are determined to overcome a handicap, nature becomes your ally and helps you to victory.
The sightless become sensitive in hearing and touch. The physically handicapped develop a versatility of other

movements and methods which the normal would neither attempt nor achieve.

Nature loves the person who will not give in! That is why no one is beaten till he decides to give in.

That he need never do and must never do, if he wants the victory.

Read Job 1: 1–5; 42: 1–6, 9–10.

CAUTION!   Day Twelve

I read in the correspondence columns of a newspaper a very wise story.

An old lady, in olden days, advertised for a new coachman. There were three applicants. She asked each of them the same question. "How near," she asked the first, "could you drive to the edge of a precipice?" He answered that he could drive within an inch of the edge.

She asked the second the same question. He also claimed that he could drive to within an inch of the edge.

She asked the third the same question. "Madam," he said, "I cannot tell you, because I always keep as far away from danger as I possibly can."

The third man got the job.

Playing with fire is a dangerous game in reality and in spiritual things.

There are things in life which have an unlimited potentiality for good or for evil. There is, for instance, human speech, as James long ago saw (Jas. 3). We can use our tongues to do great good and we can use them to work infinite harm. The tongue can persuade men to do good and seduce them to do evil; the tongue can cement friendship and bring peace in strife; the tongue can divide men in anger and destroy personal relationships. The tongue can witness to the truth and can spread all falsehood.

We must be careful how we use things which can bring blessing—or ruin—to mankind.

You will be very wise if you
  handle precious things with care;
  avoid carefully, dangerous things;
  use with care the things that can create good or evil.

"Whatsoever you do, do all to the glory of God."

Read James 3: 6–13.

NOW—AGAIN! Day Thirteen

  If with pleasure you are viewing
    any work a man is doing,
  If you like him and you trust him, tell him now.
  Don't withhold your approbation,
    till the person makes oration,
  And he lies with snowy lilies o'er his brow;
  For no matter how you shout it,
    he won't know a thing about it,
  For he cannot read his tombstone, when he's dead.

There is a law of life. There are some things you can do
and see any time; there are other things which you only get
the chance to do and see once; and if you are ever going to
see them and do them, you must take that chance, for it
does not come back.

Do you know the old Latin proverb *"qui cito dat bis dat"*?
It means "He who gives quickly gives twice".

Let us remember then some of the things to be done
quickly.

If a word of thanks should be said, say it *now*.

If a word of praise should be said, say it *now*.

If a word of encouragement should be said, say it *now*.

If that word of warning we have already mentioned should
be given, give it *now*.

If there are gifts to be given, give them *now*.

If there are decisions to be made, make them *now*.

The poet Lowell said:

Once to every man and nation comes the moment to decide,
In the strife of Truth with Falsehood, for the good or evil side.

"Choose you *this day* whom you will serve" it says in the book of Joshua.
If you don't do it now, the chance to do it may *never* return.

Read Joshua 24: 14–18.

A TINY SPARK   Day Fourteen

In Glasgow University, the famous Lord Kelvin used to illustrate the effect of small forces on large masses. In his class-room he would suspend a huge heavy lump of metal weighing as much as a hundredweight or more from the ceiling. He would also have a basket full of paper pellets; and, to the great joy of the class, he would begin to bombard the heavy iron mass with the little pellets of paper.

At first nothing happened; then after a time the iron mass would begin to tremble; then it would begin to move; and finally it would begin to swing in a wide arc, and all through the effect of repeated blows with the little paper pellets.

The little things can achieve the big things, if we keep on —but you have to keep on, for, if you stopped bombarding the iron mass with the paper pellets, it would stop moving.
It is the little, constantly repeated, efforts which count.

There is another experiment which demonstrates this. A very large beaker of clear water is taken, and a little phial of dye. Drop by drop the dye is dropped into the clear water. At first there is no alteration at all; the colour of the water remains quite unaffected. Then, bit by bit, the colour begins faintly and dimly to show; then the colour begins to darken and to deepen; and, in the end, the whole beaker of clear water is transformed into the colour of the dye.
It was drop by drop that the change was effected.

46

"Who has despised the day of small things?" said Zechariah.

"Behold how great a matter a little fire kindleth," said James.

"How great a forest fire starts from a small spark!" (as the New English Bible puts that same sentence).

Out of attention to little things, perfection comes.

Read James 3: 1–5.

DO YOUR BEST!   Day Fifteen

Perfection, I said yesterday, comes from faithful attention to little things.

But perhaps that itself is a counsel of perfection!

All we can do in the end is our best!

When Henry VIII asked Miles Coverdale to produce an English translation of the Bible, Coverdale knew very well his own limitations and his lack of the necessary scholarship in Hebrew and Greek. "Considering how excellent knowledge and learning an interpreter of Scripture ought to have in the tongues, and pondering also mine own insufficiency therein, and how weak I am to perform the office of translator, I was the more loath to meddle with this work."

But then he goes on: "But to say the truth before God, it was neither my labour nor desire to have this work put in my hand; nevertheless it grieved me that other nations should be more plenteously provided for with the Scripture in their mother tongue than we; therefore when I was instantly required, though I could not do as well as I would, I thought it my duty to do my best, and that with a good will."

He did his best.

But his best became a masterpiece!

"Be ye perfect . . ." said Jesus.

"I press toward the mark . . ." said St. Paul.

47

Do your best!
God will honour that!

Read St. Matthew 5: 38–48.

REMINDERS

I remember being in Newcastle-upon-Tyne and seeing at a very busy junction where many roads met, a monument to the famous Earl Grey of the Reform Bill. It was on a tall pillar which soared hundreds of feet into the air.

When you looked at the top of that pillar, you saw two bright shining lights outstretched on metal arms; and if you looked a little more closely, you saw there were two other arms with two unlit lights upon them.

I wondered what this meant.

It meant this.

Whenever there was a fatal road accident in Newcastle, then the two white lights were switched off and two red lights switched on. So in Newcastle they knew when someone died on the road. The red lights meant that a life had been lost.

That light was a reminder of something important.

Have you attended a Communion service, or, as some say, the Eucharist, or, as others say, the Sacrament of the Lord's Supper?

It is a reminder.

"This do in remembrance of me".

It was the same with the Passover meal for the Jews.

It was a reminder of the "exodus" from Egypt—God's act of deliverance.

So when, later in your lives, you come to share in the Lord's Supper, you will find in the symbol of the broken bread a reminder of Christ's suffering for us.

You will see in the symbol of the wine a reminder of Christ's pain for us.

"This do in remembrance of him" you will be told.
It's a reminder.
A timely reminder.

Read 1 Corinthians 11: 23–29.

FOOD BILLS   Day Seventeen

If it is money you are interested in, then don't become a priest or a preacher!
Try being a comedian, or a pop singer, or a footballer!
Even the value of Prime Ministers seems to be less than that of pop singers—at least if you look at it in terms of the money they command today!

This sort of pattern is similar to that of ancient Rome in the time of its decline and ultimate fall. It would be hard to find an age (unless it be our own!) when so much money was spent on food!
The historian Tacitus tells us of single banquets which cost as much as £500.
Seneca tells us of dinner at which the dishes included peacocks' brains and nightingales' tongues.
Suetonius tells us that the Emperor Vitellius set on the table at one banquet 2,000 fish and 7,000 birds and that in a reign of less than a year he managed to spend more than £3,000,000 on food.
The elder Pliny tells of seeing a Roman bride, Lollia Paulina, dressed in a bridal dress which was so richly jewelled that it cost £423,000.
An age which pours out money on its pleasures is a decadent age.

Extravagance is usually a sign of the desire to escape responsibility.
An age which pours out money on pleasures is almost

49

certainly one becoming decadent. It is losing its sense of values.

"What shall it profit a man if he gains the whole world and loses his soul?" asked Jesus.
It is a very good question.
Think about it!

Read Isaiah 1: 11–17.

DEMOLISHERS   Day Eighteen

There are many wall-builders in the world!
But there are too many walls.

There are people building political walls to obstruct freedom and development.
There are people building walls of hatred—bringing division through racial prejudice, or religious intolerance.
Sometimes all of us build personal walls. Perhaps it is only shyness. Perhaps it is selfishness. But we erect walls between us and others.

"Behold I stand at the door and knock," said Jesus.
In the famous picture by Holman Hunt of Jesus knocking at the door, where is the handle?
It is invisible, of course, because *it is on the inside.*
The door can only be opened from within.

It is the same with these walls.
If we wait for others to take them down, we may wait in vain.
It is for us to take the first step.

Wall-builders are useful in life—sometimes!
Our job is more that of wall-demolishers!
At least where bad walls are concerned.

Read Revelation 3: 19–22.

When William Booth, the great founder of the Salvation Army, was twenty, he drew up a list of resolutions.

Here they are.

I do promise, (he wrote), my God helping—

Firstly, that I will rise every morning sufficiently early (say twenty minutes before seven o'clock) to wash, dress and have a few minutes, not less than five, in private prayer.

Secondly, that I will, as much as possible, avoid all that babbling and idle talk in which I have lately so sinfully indulged.

Thirdly, that I will endeavour in my conduct and deportment before the world and my fellow servants especially to conduct myself as a humble, meek and zealous follower of the bleeding Lamb, and, by serious conversation and warning, endeavour to lead them to think of their immortal souls.

Fourthly, that I will not read less than four chapters in God's word every day.

Fifthly, that I will strive to live closer to God, and to seek after holiness of heart, and leave providential events with God.

Sixthly, that I will read this over every day or at least twice a week. God help me, enable me to cultivate a spirit of self-denial and to yield myself a prisoner of love to the Redeemer of the world. Amen and Amen. William Booth. I feel my own weakness, and without God's help I shall not keep these resolutions a day.

They are not a bad set of resolutions, are they?

Read Psalm 62: 1–8.

Here are some standards for you.

They lay down very essential qualities.

First there is *honesty*.

Without it, business, trade, commerce, indeed life itself, cannot go on.

If you or your word or your sincerity cannot be trusted, progress becomes impossible.

Then there is *service*.

"Whosoever seeks to save his life shall lose it, and whosoever loses his life for my sake, shall find it."

If we are *self*-centred, we will do little that contributes to life. "Give", not "get" is the word that matters to Christians.

Then there is *purity*.

It is always dangerous to be careless over the standards that affect our relationships to others. It matters how boy treats girl, and girl treats boy. Because the way boys and girls treat their relationships to each other will decide *how* valuable purity and chastity are in our world.

Have your standards.

And try to keep them.

Read St. Matthew 5: 21–30.

During the war one of the most colourful generals was an American, General Patton. He swept through Europe like a gale of wind with his pearl-handled revolver and his flair for publicity.

Someone once asked him, "How do you do it? Where on earth does the petrol come from to feed your motorised columns?" "I don't know," said Patton, "I've got a chap who looks after that."

Behind the vivid Patton there was a quiet man, whose name no one knows. But he kept the whole army moving.

The first place may be for some, but for most of us we will have to be content with the second place.

But don't despise that "second place". The man who helps is important too.

The spotlight was often on Peter, just because he was a born leader and a real personality.

It wasn't so often on Andrew, yet he played a great supporting rôle.

When some Greeks came to hear about Jesus, they came across Andrew first. And he took them to Peter . . . and on to Christ.

Do *your* bit!

Whether it is in first or second place, in the spotlight or "off stage", in the front line or as one of the "backroom boys", doesn't really matter.

It is the job itself that is all important.

"He who is faithful in little things . . ."

Read St. Matthew 25: 14–29.

IN TOUCH   Day Twenty-two

I once slept in General Montgomery's bed!

It was when I visited Ostenwalde in Germany. They assured me Montgomery had slept there!

I once, too, played football in a jersey that had been lent to me by a famous Scottish international. What a thrill it was to put over my head the jersey worn by the captain of Scotland—with *his* number on it!

Isn't it thrilling to have a personal contact with greatness?

This is, of course, the reason for our visit to museums or houses which have once belonged to famous people. To look at—and even touch—old relics gives ordinary people the thrill of a contact with greatness.

This must have been the feeling of the woman who "touched" the hem of Jesus' garment!

This must have been the great memory of the people whom Jesus touched and healed.

It is good, we say, to be "in touch" with people.
It is great to be "in touch" with God through Jesus.

"The Word became flesh and dwelt among us ..."

Read St. Matthew 9: 20–26.

JOY

What kind of face will you have in years to come?
Well it depends on what you are doing with it *now!*
For if you adopt certain expressions often, it leaves permanent marks on your face.

Have you noticed vertical lines on someone's forehead?
They are caused by constant worry!
Resentment and discontent, too, can leave marks of one kind or another.
But so too can joy!

"A happy man" said Robert Louis Stevenson, "is a better thing to find than a five pound note."

He went on: "When you looked into my mother's eyes you knew, as if he had told you, why God sent her into the world—it was to open the minds of all who looked, to beautiful thought. And that is the beginning and end of literature. These eyes that I could not see till I was six years old have guided me through life, and I pray God that they may remain my only earthly judge to the last."

His mother's face spoke of joy to him.

"Be not of a sad countenance" said Jesus, mimicking the Pharisees. They looked what they believed!

We must too—but in the right way.

Be joyful—visibly!

Read St. Luke 1: 46–55 (A song of Rejoicing).

SKIN DEEP   Day Twenty-four

There are many, many ways of putting "beauty" on your face or head—as the girls know! Creams, powders, lipsticks, mascaras, even wigs.

But this is a beauty that is only skin deep.

A famous churchman called Dean Ramsey loved to show visitors his garden. "Come into my garden," he would say, "I would like you to see my roses."

But one day a very beautiful lady called.

"Come into my garden" said the Dean, "I would like my roses to see you!"

The girls would love a compliment like that, wouldn't they?

But is beauty only to be skin deep? Or is true beauty something more than this? An "inner" beauty—that is of much more value?

Beauty that is only skin deep is very temporary. It comes off at night and goes on again in the morning. It is designed primarily to impress others.

The beauty that is really important is of a totally different kind. It has quality and permanence.

Make it your aim to find the things which are "good and lovely and of good report."

These are the things that matter.

Read St. Luke 6: 40–45.

Christopher Columbus would not take "No" for an answer. For eighteen years he tramped round the courts and the great houses seeking financial help to fit out a squadron to discover the new worlds on the other side of the seas.

Booker Washington wanted a university education. He heard of a college which would accept Negroes. He walked there, hundreds of miles. When he arrived there, the college was full up; but he pleaded so hard that they gave him a job sweeping the floors and making the beds and cleaning the windows, and in the end he got in as a student, because he would not take "No" for an answer.

Once, seeking to find a way to do something, he carried out more than seven hundred experiments, all of which ended in failure. "Now", he said cheerfully, "we know seven hundred ways not to do it," and carried on until he got the right way.

There is a story in the New Testament of a woman who would not take "No" for an answer. She wanted Jesus to heal her sick daughter (Mark 7: 24-30); but she was not a Jew and Jesus' mission was in the first place to the Jews, and he told her that his help was not at the moment for her. "You can't take the children's bread," he said, "and throw it to the dogs." "True," she replied, "but, sir, even the dogs under the table eat the children's scraps!" "For saying that," said Jesus, "you may go home content." And she went home to find her daughter healed.

Ask . . . and you will receive.
Seek . . . and you will find.
Knock . . . and it will be opened to you.
But keep asking, seeking, knocking.

As in the parable of the importunate widow in the New Testament, things will happen if you don't take "No" for an answer.

Read St. Mark 7: 24-30.

There is an old Roman story which tells how one of the Emperors was celebrating a triumph and was leading his victorious troops through the streets of Rome.

The streets were crowded with people, and at a certain point on the route a platform had been erected from which the Empress and Emperor's family might see this scene.

The route was lined with great tall Roman legionaries, fully armed. When the procession was coming near the platform where the Empress and the children were, the Emperor's little son jumped down off the platform, burrowed his way through the crowd and was just about to run out on the road to intercept his father's imperial chariot.

One of the legionaries who were lining the road, picked him up and held him. "You can't run out there," he said "Don't you know who that is who is just about to ride by? That's the Emperor. You can't run out to him."

The little lad laughed at the legionary. "He may be your Emperor," he said, "but he's my father."

Labels and titles are sometimes very important in the world's eyes. But real relationships in life are formed when people are themselves.

"The rank is but the guinea's stamp, the man's the gowd for a' that" said Robert Burns.

Be yourself. This is what "integrity" means.

So much goes wrong in life because we pretend. Indeed the word "hypocrite" which Jesus used so often about people who pretended goodness means "play actor".

"I love you for yourself alone ..." says the poet in another connection.

So does God.

He is not interested in your status, reputation, fame or popularity.

Be yourself!

Read James 2: 1–9.

In the primitive districts of India there are, of course, no lights in the streets or in the houses. The only lighting is made by simple little oil lamps, like the ones people were using when Jesus lived in the flesh.

In one of these country districts of India is a temple. And hanging from the roof of it there is a great brass structure with one hundred different places into which these little lamps may fit. Until the lamps are put into it the temple is dark.

But, as each worshipper comes and places his lamp, bit by bit the temple grows lighter and lighter, until, when all the hundred places are filled with the lamps which the worshippers bring, the temple is a blaze of light.

This is a parable of how a church service should be. It is not the minister or priest or preacher that makes the service, but everyone who comes to worship. The worship is made up of the contributions of all.

Is there eagerness or listlessness in the church you attend?
Is there a warm atmosphere or a cold one?
Is there a friendly atmosphere or an unfriendly one?
The kind of worship a church has depends on the answers to these questions.
And of course the answer lies in what we do about it!

"Let *your* light shine . . ."

Read St. John 8: 12–18.

THE PROPHET   Day Twenty-eight

Prophets had a great part to play in the Old Testament.
What is a prophet?
Someone who foretells the future?

The prophet is not a fortune teller, foretelling coming events.

He is the man who understands and interprets the meaning and significance of *present* events, especially in moral terms.

He does this because—
 He has the ability to see more deeply than others:
 He has a capacity to hear, because he has learned to listen;
 He has the courage to speak out about what he sees and hears;
 He is able to do this because he is a dedicated man.

"Here am I! Send me," said Isaiah.
"Speak, Lord, for thy servant hears," said Samuel.
You can see why these men became prophets.

Read Isaiah 6: 1–8.

IN PART   Day Twenty-nine

Once Buddha was in a town where there was a conflict of warring theological views between the monks. Some believed one thing and some another, and each of them believed that he alone was right.

So Buddha told them the parable of the Rajah, the blind men and the elephant.

One day the Rajah called a servant, and bade him assemble at his palace, all the men in the town who had been born blind. Then he commanded that an elephant should be brought in. The Rajah made one blind man touch the head of the elephant, another the ear, another the trunk, a tusk, a foot, the back, the tail, and the tuft of the tail; and to each one the Rajah said that he was touching the elephant.

When they had all felt the elephant, the Rajah said to them, "Have you all studied the elephant? Now tell me your conclusions."

The man who had touched the head said, "It is like a pot." The one who had touched the ear said, "It is like a fan."

And for the others the trunk became a plough; a tusk, a ploughshare; a foot, a pillar; the back, a granary; the tail, a pestle; the tuft of the tail, a besom.

Each blind man thought that the bit he had touched was an elephant.

They began therefore to argue with each other and to quarrel, saying, "An elephant is like this"—"No, it is like this"—"I tell you it is not"—and so on until, in the end, they came to blows.

That, said the Buddha, is what men are like about the truth.

We all want to say that the bit of truth we know is the whole truth.

Churches have done this too often.
Political parties are always doing it.
Leaders of different religions have done it.

"What is truth?" asked Pilate.
That is a very big question.
But we can be sure it is more than the bit we know.

As an Indian guru said in a parable about mountain-climbers: "You don't get the view from the foot of the mountain. It is only from the top, you see the whole picture."

Perhaps how we get to the truth is less important than finding it.

Read 1 Corinthians 13: 9–12.

MONTH THREE

BEAUTY FROM A BLOT

A story is told of John Ruskin, the famous art critic and artist.

One day a lady, who was a friend of his, showed him a handkerchief made of very precious material. A blot of indelible ink had fallen upon it, and the lady was lamenting to Ruskin that the very valuable handkerchief was ruined beyond repair.

Ruskin asked if he might have it. The lady said that of course he could have it, but she could not see why he should want the ruined piece of material.

Some days later Ruskin brought the handkerchief back, and on it, beginning from the blot, and making the blot the centre of the whole matter, Ruskin had drawn the most intricate and beautiful design.

Out of the unlikely and the unpleasant, beauty had come.

Paul had "a thorn in the flesh". What it was we are not sure, but it was probably some kind of illness—like epilepsy, or migraine. Through that thorn, Paul says he learned about "the grace which is sufficient for us".

"I have learnt more of God since I came to this bed than in all my life before," said the Scottish preacher, Robert Leighton. Illness is an unpleasant thing, but it can often help us to see what really matters.

So just as God can use pain to help us, he can use sorrow or hardship to help us too.

He was even able to turn the suffering of the Cross into a blessing for everyone.

Read Psalm 130.

TROUBLE AHEAD!

Garibaldi, the liberator of Italy, after the siege of Rome

in 1849 issued the following proclamation: "Soldiers, all our efforts against superior forces have been unavailing. I have nothing to offer you but hunger and thirst, hardship and death; but I call on all who love their country to join with me."

They joined in their hundreds.

When Jesus says "Follow me", he makes it quite clear that to be a disciple involves cost.

"Come, follow me" he said to the men of his time. "And I will make you fishers of men" (Matt. 4: 19).

There was a job to do.

He sent his disciples out with a warning that there was trouble ahead (Matt. 10: 5–42).

He left them a responsibility—to be "witnesses" to him (Acts 1: 8). That could not be easy.

Christianity involves making a stand.

It may be on a matter of principle.

It may be on a question of personal policy.

It may involve the need to be different, to refuse to conform to what others do.

Yes, Jesus does say "Follow me".

It does mean, for those who do, that there may be trouble ahead.

Read St. John 21: 15–23.

THE GIFTS THAT COUNT   Day Three

Paul was quite certainly not a handsome man. In the third-century work called the *Acts of Paul and Thecla*, there is a description of Paul which is so unflattering that it must be genuine: "A man of little stature, thin-haired upon the head, crooked in the legs, of good state of body, with eyebrows joining and nose somewhat hooked."

No one would have looked twice at Paul for his looks!

Still further, strangely enough, it seems that Paul was not even a very good speaker, and that he was certainly no orator. The Corinthians said of him that "his bodily presence is weak, and his speech of no account" (2 Cor. 10: 10).

You don't have to be beautiful or handsome to do God's work. You don't even have to be a good speaker. The Corinthians made that clear!

There was a very famous preacher called Thomas Chalmers who played a great part in history. Yet far from being an orator, history records that he never lifted his head from his manuscript, and even followed each line with his finger as he read what he had to say.

On top of that, he spoke in a broad local dialect that must have sounded strange to many.

If you are handsome or beautiful or a good public speaker, be grateful and dedicate these gifts to God! But it you are not (and few of us can claim such talents), don't think it stops you being God's man or woman, boy or girl.

Sincerity and love are the gifts that count.

Read 2 Corinthians 10: 7–18.

THE TRULY GREAT! Day Four

One of the greatest castles in England is Arundel Castle, and one of the greatest of all English aristocracy is the Duke of Norfolk to whom that castle belongs.

Once a certain Duke of Norfolk happened to be at the railway station, when a little Irish girl arrived off the train with a very heavy bag. She had come to be a maidservant at the castle.

The castle is about a mile from the station and the little

Irish girl was trying to persuade a porter to carry her heavy bag to the castle, for which she offered him a shilling, all the money that she had. The porter contemptuously refused. The Duke stepped forward, shabby as usual in appearance. He offered to carry her bag, took it and walked beside her along the road to the castle, talking to her.

At the end of the journey, he gratefully accepted the shilling she offered him, never allowing her to know who he was; and it was only the next day, when she met her employer, that the little Irish girl knew that the Duke of Norfolk had carried her bag from the station to the castle and that she had tipped him a shilling!

A very wonderful story of a true nobleman that tells us a good many things about this kind of man!

Never judge a man by his possessions.
The truly great man is not interested in status or prestige.
The great man is a thoughtful man.
To be able to receive graciously is as great a quality as giving graciously.

Truly great people find it is never humiliating to serve anyone.
As Jesus proved.

Read St. Mark 10: 35–45.

LEARNING. LIGHT. LAUGHTER Day Five

You can learn a lot about people from the books they read.

One morning, I was coming across from our main University buildings in Glasgow to the Divinity Hall, Trinity College, with four other members of our staff in my car. We reached Trinity College, and as we were getting out of the car one of my passengers began to laugh. "Just look

66

what you've got lying on your back window ledge," he said. And lying on the back window ledge there was a copy of Karl Barth's commentary on *Philippians*, a copy of the A.A. *Roadbook of England and Wales*—and two comics called *Judy* and *Bunty*, which my daughter Jane had left in the car.

My friend was rather amused by this particular "library"! But I thought it was a very good selection.

There was a book to *teach*.
There was a book to *guide*.
There were the comics to *amuse*.
Learning, Light and Laughter!
There is not much wrong with this combination, is there?

Learning

I entered Trinity College as a student in 1929, which means that the study of the Bible, and in particular the New Testament, has been the main activity of my life for thirty-three years, and I still find that there are so many things about it to know and to learn, and so many things of absorbing interest of which I have touched only the fringes, and so many things which I have not yet studied at all. There is a limitless quality about Scripture.

Light

We need light and guidance, and of course the Bible exists to give just that.
"Thy word is a lamp," says the Psalmist.
It is.

Laughter?

Yes, the Bible has a word to say that makes it a good thing to do.
"There is a time to laugh," it says.

Read St. John 3: 16–21.

Why do you yawn?
There are three reasons.
We yawn:
    when we are tired.
    when we are bored.
    when we are hungry.
"He giveth his beloved sleep" it says in the Bible.
Sleep is a wonderful thing.
It is the most healing and renewing thing we do.
Not to be able to sleep is a terrible curse.

Jesus said: (as the New English Bible has it) "Come to me all those whose work is hard, whose load is heavy, and I will give you relief" (Matt. 11: 28).

When he was nearly eighty and still travelling, writing, and speaking, John Wesley said he did not know what it was to be tired.
Jesus gives rest.

Hungry?
Is that why you yawn?
Does that also mean spiritual yawning is the sign of spiritual hunger?
"I am the bread of life," said Jesus. "He that comes to me shall not hunger and he who believes in me shall not thirst" (John 6: 35).
"Blessed are they that hunger and thirst after righteousness."
Jesus gives food for the soul.

Bored?
"I am come that they might have life, and have it abundantly" (John 10: 10).
Jesus gives life.

Read St. Matthew 11: 25–30.

A man is like a watch!

A watch counts the hours.
So should we, if we are sensible.
"So teach us to number our days, that we may apply our hearts to wisdom" (Ps. 90: 12).
Use the hours.

A watch keeps time.
Be punctual!
"Punctuality," someone has said, "is the politeness of princes."
Unpunctuality is discourtesy.
It is the breaking of a trust, a promise.
Don't waste the hours.

A watch regulates the hours.
The wise man similarly doesn't hurry or linger.
To be always rushing is not the best way to get things done.
To plod along wearily is to do less than we can.

"The Lord is my pace-setter," says a Japanese version of the Twenty-third Psalm.
Keep in step!

Read Isaiah 50: 4–10.

MORE ABOUT A WATCH   Day Eight

A watch has a mainspring.
It is that spring that keeps it going.
The wise man finds his strength is within himself too.

"I have learned to find resources within myself" says the New English Bible version of Paul's words about true contentment.

A watch that goes wrong has to be returned to its maker.
And people? What do they do?
Surely, the same.
Return to God to get help there.

God, says the Bible, "is a very present help in trouble".
He is "our refuge and our strength".
He is, indeed.

Read Psalm 46.

BE TOLERANT

I once visited that amazing parish church in Boston in Lincolnshire. It has one of the largest parish churches in all England.

Boston is still busy, but compared with what it once was, it is a little place. But there was a time when Boston was second as a seaport only to London, and still that famous tower, Boston Stump, stretches 275 feet into the sky, a landmark for miles around and a guide to the sailor at sea.

They say of Boston church that it is built in a very special way. They say that there are seven doors to stand for the seven days of the week; twelve pillars in the nave to stand for the twelve months; twenty-four steps to the library to stand for the hours of the day; fifty-two windows to stand for the weeks of the year; sixty steps to the chancel roof to stand for the seconds in a minute; 365 steps to the top of the tower, to stand for the days of the year. So if you know the way that Boston church is built, you cannot look at it without remembering the passing of time.

I am not ancient, but I would seem old to you! You are young and are not conscious of the passing of time. But I have found there are certain ways in which I have benefited from growing older.

I am much more sympathetic than I was once.
Perhaps it is because time brings loss and suffering that I can feel sympathy with others who suffer.

But you don't need to be as old as I am to develop sympathy and understanding.

You can start doing it at *your* age.

So do that from now!

I am much more tolerant than I was.

It is very easy to be intolerant when we are young. We think we know everything! We think we are always right!

Take it from me that we don't know everything, ever. We can be wrong.

So if it has taken me a long time to learn it, don't feel *you* have to wait till you are my age to do so!

You can learn to be tolerant and understanding *now*!

Read I Thessalonians 5: 14–23.

WE NEED ... Day Ten

"Without me, you can do nothing" Jesus said (John 15: 5).

I believe this is true in several ways.

We need divine help to guide us in what we ought to do.

We need that help to give us the courage to do what is right.

We need help in seeing things through, right to the end.

We need help in times of temptation.

To do what we ought to do?

Yes, our prejudices and personal wishes may lead us to wrong decisions. Only in his light, do we see the light (Ps. 36: 9).

To give us courage?

It is not easy to stand alone. We are, by nature, *happiest* in groups. As a result we tend to do what others do.

71

So standing up for something, on our own is not easy.
We need help.

Getting to the end?
"Keep right on to the end of the road", says the old
Scottish song. But it isn't always easy to keep going.
Again we need help.

To fight temptation?
Jesus was tempted—"like as we are" says the Bible.
So he can help, just because he knows what it is like.

"Without me, you can do nothing".
"With me, all things are possible."

Read St. John 15: 1–8.

BEFORE WE ASK ...   Day Eleven

Here are some more things about prayer for your thinking.

There is no time when you cannot go to God in prayer.
In that lovely psalm about lifting up our eyes to the hills,
it tells us that God "neither slumbers nor sleeps" (as we
said before).
God is never off duty!
He does not work office hours.
He is always there.

There is nothing too little to take to God.
"If a thing is big enough to worry about, it is big enough
to pray about," said the distinguished theologian, Dr. John
Baillie.
Something that seems trivial to people in general may be
very important to you. If it is important to you, it will be
important to God. But in any case it is valuable to take it to
God because there you get things in proportion and you
will realise just how important—or unimportant—it is.

72

There is nothing too shameful to take to God.

God knows our innermost thoughts. So he knows "before we ask" what is on our minds.

Because nothing can surprise him, nothing will shock him. In other words, he will understand.

Yes, as the old hymn says, "take it to the Lord in prayer".

Read Psalm 121.

STAY ALIVE!   Day Twelve

A letter came to me from a lady who had been a teacher in one of Glasgow's most famous schools for girls. After a long and honourable career, she had come to the age when she retired. And now she was well over sixty years of age.

The letter said that all her life this lady had wanted to study the New Testament in Greek. Now that she was retired, she had time to do so. So she made a request— would she be allowed to attend the class of Hellenistic Greek as a student on the benches?

There was only one answer to that; it would be a pleasure and a privilege to have her. And so this lady of over sixty sat on the benches of a University class-room, listening and taking notes with students a third of her age.

This is a magnificent example.

It is never too late to learn.

Cato lived in the days of the Roman Empire when Greek culture was invading Rome, and at the age of eighty he set himself to learn Greek.

At the age of seventy, Corot, the great painter, said, "If God spares me for another ten years, I think I may learn to paint."

Mozart was never an old man in years, for he died all too young. But when he was famous and one of the great ones even in his own lifetime, he was even then taking lessons in counterpoint and musical theory.

At the age of ninety Sir William Mulock, the Lord Chief

Justice of Canada, said, "The best is yet to be, hidden beyond the hills of time."

If you want to stay alive, keep learning.
One of the tragedies of life is that there are so many people who are physically alive, but who are mentally and spiritually dead.

Read St. John 3: 1–7.

WELCOME! Day Thirteen

"We welcome you to our Church and Fellowship and extend Christian greetings to you."

When I read this notice in a pew at Martyrs' Church in St. Andrews, I felt I was among friends.

I was no more a stranger.

After the service I told one of the office-bearers what a fine idea I thought this was, and how much I personally had appreciated it, and he at once went on to tell me about two other cards which Martyrs' Church uses.

The first is put into the pews on Communion Sundays and it runs:

"The minister, kirk session and congregation of Martyrs' Church, St. Andrews, welcome you to the fellowship of the Lord's Table."

I know how touched I would have been to find that card in my pew had I happened to come to Martyrs' on a Communion Sunday.

But perhaps the third card is the most original of all. It is a card which the members of Martyrs' Church take with them when they go to other congregations, for instance when they are away on holiday, and it runs:

"As a visitor to this Church, I bring warm Christian greetings to all who worship here from Martyrs' Church, St. Andrews."

And the members of Martyrs' Church leave that card in the churches in which they happen to worship.

I don't know who first thought of all this, and I certainly don't know how many other churches may do it, but it is a splendid idea.

As you grow older, why not encourage things like this in *your* church?

Read Psalm 122.

A FAIR DEMAND Day Fourteen

Our Christian faith makes great claims.
Think of these for example:
It claims to be *the religion of peace.*
It claims to be *the religion of service.*
It claims to be *the religion of power.*
It claims to be *the religion of love.*
It claims to be *the religion of forgiveness.*

How do Christians "make out" on these claims? Not too well.

There are too many of us who are joy-less in our attitudes and that is just not good enough.

There are many situations in the churches where there is division rather than peace. *That* is not good enough.

Christians do not always demonstrate what the Bible calls "the power of the Spirit". They should!

Christians do not always serve others freely and without ulterior motive. But they ought to!

Do we love one another? truly?

Do we forgive others? truly?

The famous German philosopher Nietzsche, who was not a Christian, said:

"Show me that you are redeemed, and then I will believe in your redeemer."

It is a fair demand.

Read St. Matthew 5: 13–16.

WHY CHURCH? Day Fifteen

Why should you go to church?

Here is one answer.

There are certain things in life which gain in value from being experienced *with others*.

An orchestra *can* play well on its own. But an audience adds something valuable.

A football team *can* play happily with the gates shut, but a match really comes to life when the spectators crowd in.

Christian worship is like that.

We *can* worship alone.

Sometimes it is even good to do this. But what a difference when two or three—or more—worship together!

There is also great value in knowing that what we believe is not just a personal opinion, but belongs to a whole community of people.

In very early days, the creed—that is the official statement of the Church's faith—began not "I believe ..." but "We believe ..."

It gives *us* encouragement to know what we believe is in fact the faith of the *whole* Church.

Yes, we need the Church.

And the Church needs us!

Read Acts 2: 41–47.

OPPORTUNITIES Day Sixteen

Grasp the opportunity, whatever it is!

This is a valuable piece of advice; for opportunities missed may mean opportunities for our growth that will never come again. So take opportunities when they come, and use them for good.

For example—

If a performance is given—musical, dramatic or whatever—do you jump at the chance to criticise, or do you look for an opportunity to give credit?

Do you encourage or discourage?

If someone suggests a bold course of action, what do you do? Try to persuade them it is impossible? Or encourage them to take a calculated risk?

Do you "count your blessings" or tot up your misfortunes?

The famous psychologist, Alfred Adler, tells of two men each of whom lost an arm.

At the end of a year one of them was so discouraged that he decided life was not worth living with a handicap like that. The other was so happy that he went about saying that he really did not know why nature had given him two arms when he could get along perfectly with one!

Do you say thanks for what you have, or blame God for what you haven't?

Sir John Reith, the first director of the BBC, said: "I do not like crises, but I do like the opportunities they bring."

It's worth thinking about that statement!

Read 1 Kings 19: 1–21.

THANKS TO CHRISTIANITY   Day Seventeen

Hasn't Christianity brought about wonderful things?

For example this.

There was no such thing as a hospital until Christianity came. The care of the aged, the sick and the poor began as Christian undertakings.

Aristotle, the Greek philosopher, said when laying down the law for his "ideal state": "Let there be a law that no deformed child shall be reared."

The writer Varro in giving rules for farming, advises that any aged slave who is past working, should be thrown out and left to die—as if he were a broken implement.

Look what happened in Nazi Germany. Christianity was banished: the aged died in gas chambers: Jews were tortured; the poor and the sick were used for medical experiments.

We ought to be grateful for Christianity!

For example again.

We owe the right of free speech and the freedom to follow conscience to Christianity. Because Christianity puts value on individuals, it encourages their freedom and their development.

You have only to look at a country like Russia to see what happens under a Communist régime. Opposition and criticism are just not allowed.

We ought to value this right to speak that Christianity has won for us.

And because we value the products of a Christian civilisation, we must do all we can to maintain Christian ways and uphold Christian values.

Read 1 John 4: 7–19.

CHRISTIANS OUGHT ...   Day Eighteen

A Christian is someone who ought to be able to do things others can't do.

I know a man who applied for an important job, but didn't get it. So what did he do immediately? He wrote to the man who got the job to congratulate him on doing so!

I mention this because I find many Christians can't stand

disappointment. They are "bad losers". They become bitter at their own failures and others' success.

As James says (in another connection!), "My brothers, these things ought not to be".

They shouldn't!

The Christian should be able to cope with disappointment *better* than the non-Christian.

Similarly Christians ought to be able to bear sorrows and burdens better than others can.

There is a curious story told of a Bishop Quayle, an American bishop.

For years he worried about his church, his staff, his work and many other things.

One night, as he sat worrying, he says he heard God's voice as clearly as if it had come from someone sitting in the room. "Quayle," said the voice, "you go to bed. I'll sit up for the rest of the night!"

That, says Bishop Quayle, taught me to "cast my burdens on the Lord" and learn true peace and serenity.

Yes, the Christian should, more than others, know that sense of peace.

Read Isaiah 40: 25–31.

ALMOST ...   Day Nineteen

It is easy in life to linger too long in the vestibule.

"Lingering in the vestibule" can happen in quite a lot of ways.

Perhaps you have heard someone preaching or lecturing. You are waiting with interest for them to get to the heart of their subject, but they never get there! They spend all their time giving the historical background, setting the subject in context and so on. The real thing is never reached!

This sometimes happens in studying, even in studying the Bible.

To get to the heart of anything needs disciplined study and patience. This means hard work and real concentration.

It is all too easy to "linger in the vestibule" and never reach the real riches. And this is certainly true of study of the Bible.

This is sometimes true in friendship. We know many boys and girls very casually, but true friendship is more than that. It means getting to know people in a much deeper way.

This means effort. It often, too, means refusing to be put off by things you don't like about other people. But it is worth trying. The real value in friendship is the giving of your whole self and the receiving of that from someone else.

We sometimes linger in the vestibule in getting to know Jesus.

"You think it will not take much to win me over and make a Christian of me", said Agrippa to Paul (Acts 26: 28).

Almost . . .

There spoke the man who stopped in the vestibule.

Read Acts 26: 24–32.

USE YOUR YEARS! Day Twenty

You cannot measure the value of a life in terms of years.

Think on these people—some of whom I have mentioned to you already.

Alexander the Great died at thirty-three.

John Keats the poet died at twenty-six.

Another poet, Rupert Brooke, died at twenty-eight.

Franz Schubert, the great musician, died at thirty-one.

Mozart, that other great musician, died at thirty-six.

Just think what these men did in the comparatively few

years they had. Alexander the Great, to take but one, literally changed the face of the world in that time!

And what about Jesus himself?
He was only in his early thirties when he died.
But look what *he* did!

It is not *how long* we live that matters.
It is what we do with our years that counts.

So "remember your Creator in the days of your youth", (which is now!) and it will condition all that you do with the coming years.

For it is the use to which you put those years that will make you a blessing to the world.

Read Ecclesiastes 12: 1–7.

LIVELY STONES   Day Twenty-one

Shape thyself for use;
The stone that may fit in the wall is left not in the way,
Then may fate thy measure take and say;
I find thee worthy;
Do this deed for me.

I saw this inscription dated 1897 on a stone in a wall in a place called Dinnet near Aberdeen. It had to do with Queen Victoria.

The stone that is shapeless is useless.
The stone that has a shape can be used and will be fitted into something of lasting value.
Isn't this a parable of life?

Peter had a wonderful vision of us as "living stones". In the building of life, we have our place.
The place *we* occupy matters.

There is a place for you in the world.
Or, if you like, God has a purpose for *you*.

But suppose you try fitting stories together without preparation—shaping them to occupy the right place! It will not work.

The mason's hammer and chisel must mould and form it to fill the place it is going to occupy.

It is the shaping that counts.

If you and I are to be "living stones" we need shaping.
That God will do.
If we let him.

Read 1 Peter 2: 1–10.

THE REAL YOU   Day Twenty-two

Did you read about the man who became a criminal and was sent to jail? While he was "inside", he tamed, by sheer patience and love, a magpie!

It took time to win that bird's trust.
But he did.

Which do you think was the real man there?
The cruel criminal or the tender bird-lover?
It is a good question, isn't it?

Which was the real Peter?
The one who denied Jesus three times or the one who took his life in his hands for Jesus before the Sanhedrin (the Jewish authorities)? (Acts 4: 8–12).

Which was the real John?
The one who wanted to call down fire from heaven to destroy a Samaritan village or the one who had but one message: "Little children, love one another"?

Which is the real me?
I can work very hard: but I can be lazy.
I can be generous, yet I can be mean and selfish.
I can be kind, but I can be cruel.
Sometimes I am very patient, yet at other times I am very impatient.

So which is the real person?
It's worth thinking a little more about this.

Read St. Matthew 16: 13–20.

A NEW CREATION   Day Twenty-three

Let's just look at this matter of our "two natures" again.

The Jews said that inside every one of us there are two natures—the *Yetser Hatoh*, the good nature, and the *Yetser Hara*, the evil nature. They said that every man had two angels, a good angel on his right hand pulling him up, and a bad angel on his left hand dragging him down.

Socrates said the soul was like a charioteer with the task of driving two horses, one gentle and tame, the other wild and undisciplined. One represented the passions, the other the reason.

Do you remember the famous chapter in the letter to the Romans (it is chapter 7) where Paul talks about the problem of the two natures he felt he had?

Listen to him: "What I do is the wrong which is against my will" (Romans 7: 19).

There is an old and famous story called *Dr. Jekyll and Mr. Hyde.* Do you know it? It is a brilliant effort to show in a dramatic form this strange fact about life.

How can we control the evil side of us and make the good side supreme?

St. Paul had no problems with *his* answer.

It was Jesus.

That's what he meant when he said that a man who is "in Christ" is a "new creation".

In the Christian the good is winning!

Read Romans 6: 11–18.

A MERRY HEART

A merry heart and a happy face!
These are the things God wants to see in his followers.

The writer of the Proverbs has a saying which the Authorised Version translates: "A merry heart doeth good like a medicine" (Prov. 17: 22). But, if we look in the margin, we find another translation: "A merry heart doeth good to a medicine." Moffat has: "A glad heart helps and heals" and the American Revised Standard Version has: "A cheerful heart is a good medicine."

Medicine will do far more good to a man with a happy heart than it will to a gloomy, pessimistic patient.

Perhaps the doctor should write on his prescriptions: "To be taken three times a day with a merry heart"!

Those who laugh most live longest!
This is, medically, not far from truth. Laughter expands the lungs, so does you good.

To be happy is to do ourselves good.

To be happy is also to do good to others.
People seem to find it difficult to connect joy and worship. But listen to these words from Job: "The morning stars sang together and all the sons of God shouted for joy". Why? because God had created the world.

"Sing unto the Lord," says the Psalmist. How right this is!

To meet someone and feel better for it is a tribute to that person.
Let us all be happy and in doing that, help others.

Read St. Matthew 6: 16–21.

Grenfell of Labrador once came to Johns Hopkins University in America looking for a nurse to go to Labrador to help with the work there.

This is how he put it: "If you want to have the time of your life, come with me and run a hospital next summer for the orphans of the Northland. There will not be a cent of money in it for you, and you will have to pay your own expenses. But I'll guarantee you will feel a love for life you have never before experienced. It's having the time of anyone's life to be in the service of Christ."

Now there is a prescription for happiness!

One of the stories in the New Testament is that of the turning of the water into wine at the marriage feast in Cana in Galilee (John 2: 1-11).

Whatever else that story means, and however we are to take it, one thing is quite certain. It means that whenever and wherever Jesus comes into life, there comes into life with him a new exhilaration, which is like turning water into wine.

There is a sort of justice in life!

Jesus put it this way: "Whatever measure you deal out to others, will be dealt back to you" (Matt. 7: 2). As we are to others, so they will be to us.

Gloom creates gloom.

Joy produces joy.

It is said that we must "take people as we find them".

It is also true that we make people what we find them.

Read St. John 2: 1-11.

CONFIDENCE Day Twenty-six

When the famous French writer Balzac was a boy, he told his father he would give his life to writing and be an author.

Balzac was worried about the risk he was going to take in doing this.

"If you become an author," he said, "and if you take literature as your career, you will be either a beggar or a king."

"In that case," said his son, "I will be a king."

That is confidence!

When Admiral Cunningham was a schoolboy, his father wrote to him asking him if he would like to enter the Navy. An opening had arisen and he could have it.

"Yes," his son wrote back, "I would like to be an Admiral."

That is confidence!

Confidence is right and good when you feel you have gifts and talents and are ready to fight hard to achieve success.
If you feel like that, aim for high service!

But beware the arrogant self-confidence that is only a form of wrong pride.
This is never good or right.

Read St. Luke 9: 46–48.

THE IMPOSSIBLE   **Day Twenty-seven**

Edison, the inventor, said that the only difference between the difficult and the impossible is that the impossible takes a little longer!

General Wingate, who was known for his bravery in Burma in the Second World War, once issued an extraordinary "order of the day" to his troops. It read:
"No jungle shall be reported to be impenetrable until it has been penetrated."

Sometimes things look very discouraging at a distance, and probably impossible. But go closer and try harder, and the "impossible" may not be so impossible!

"Don't worry about tomorrow. Let tomorrow worry about itself," said Jesus. "Each day has troubles enough of it own" (Matt. 6: 34).

No one really knows how much he can stand until he has to bear it. It is obvious that the heart can stand enormous stresses and yet not break—just think what athletes do at Olympic Games.

Heroism in life is often the occasion when men show that they can do the impossible.

Life will bring its tests for you.
They will look ominous!
But it is amazing how much you can stand and do—with God's help.

Read 1 Samuel 30: 1–6.

COLOUR-BLIND   Day Twenty-eight

Are you colour-blind?
No, I don't mean literally (some people are, of course).
I mean in terms of race prejudice.

The answer is you are!
I say this because I have found that so far as racial intolerance is concerned, boys and girls are truly colour-blind.

At least I find this to be true of all the children I have met in Britain. (It may be more difficult in countries where this is a family problem from birth of course.)

What I am really saying is that the development of colour prejudice is a grown-up's sin. It is just not natural in children who take each other for what they are, not for what they look like.

God is colour-blind.

He is (as James says) "no respecter of persons".

There is (as Jesus says) "one fold and one shepherd".

There is no difference in the eyes of God (as Paul says) between Jew and Greek, male and female, bond or free: and I think we could add black and white.

"God so loved *the world*".

Not the white bits of it.

But all of it and all in it.

We must too.

Read St. Luke 10: 25–37.

THE PADRE   Day Twenty-nine

I wonder if any of you boys might ever become an army chaplain—or Padre, as he is often known.

What are the qualities you would need to undertake this work?

You would need to be interested in people.

Paul Tournier in *A Doctor's Casebook* speaks of what he calls the modern "massification" of society. The tendency nowadays is for the individual to be lost in the mass. It is so easy for the individual to cease in any sense to be an individual, and become a number on a form, an entry on a file, a specimen pigeon-holed in some neat classification. Paul Tournier says that the doctor's great danger is that he ceases to think of a man as a person, and begins to think of him as a gall-bladder or a lung case.

Sydney Carter (who wrote *Lord of the Dance*) has written an amusing poem called "Zero One" in which he refers to the change from telephone exchanges in London with *letters* to *numbers* only. Even so, TIM (for the time) is now just 123!

He makes this the chorus:

All the names have got to go
Banished by the G.P.O.
For numbers rule the world today
You and I are in the way.

The Padre must never think of people as just numbers.
After all Jesus says, "Even the hairs of your head are
numbered."

The Padre must share the soldiers' problems.
Ezekiel said this: "I sat where they sat" (Ezek. 3: 15).
This is what we all have to do—be beside people in their
difficulties.
Could you do that?

The Padre must be a bridge builder.
The word *pontifex* in Latin means priest, a bridge-
builder.
The priest is a bridge-builder.
He builds bridges between God and men and between
one man and another.

All this is well worth doing.
Might *you* think about it?

Read Hebrews 5: 1–10.

A JOY FOREVER   Day Thirty

The famous Scottish preacher, Dr. A. J. Gossip, used to
love to tell a story about Mungo Park, the great explorer.
He had been journeying for days and miles in the wilds of
China, in the most desolate surroundings. Then quite
suddenly he saw on the ground at his feet a little blue
flower. And, as he saw it, he said gently, "God has been
here!"

There is so much beauty in the world.
The sky and the clouds . . .

89

The heavens which "declare God's handiwork . . ."
The smile of a baby . . .
Friendship . . .

Beauty should do three things for us.

First, it should remind us of God himself.
To see beauty is to be more aware of the world as God's
world. Not even all the wrong-doing that is in the world can
destroy that.

Second, it should make us grateful—for the gift of beauty
is something for which to say thanks.

Third, it should move us to action, so that we want to
create beauty in whatever way we can—with our hands, our
lips, our brains . . .

"A thing of beauty is a joy for ever."
Not least because it leads us to God.

Read Psalm 23.

POWER IN THE WORD   Day Thirty-one

Tokichi Ishii had a record of savage and beastly cruelty
that was almost without equal. With almost fiendish bru-
tality he had murdered men, women and even children, and
had pitilessly and cold-bloodedly removed anyone who stood
in his way. At last the law caught up with him. He was
captured; he was in prison awaiting execution.

While he was in prison, he was visited by two Canadian
ladies who tried to talk to him through the prison bars. They
were unable to make even the very slightest impression on
him. He merely glowered back at them like a wild animal.

In the end they left a Bible with him, in the faint hope that
the Bible might be able to make the appeal that no human
words had been able to make.

Then it happened. He began to read, and the story so
gripped him that he could not stop. He read on until he

came at last to the story of the Crucifixion. It was the words, "Father, forgive them, for they know not what they do," that broke down his last resistance. "I stopped," he said. "I was stabbed to the heart, as if pierced by a five-inch nail. Shall I call it the love of Christ? Shall I call it his compassion? I do not know what to call it. I only know that I believed and that the hardness of my heart was changed."

Later, says A. M. Chirgwin, as he retells the story in *The Bible in World Evangelism*, when the jailer came to lead the doomed man to the scaffold, he found, not the surly, hardened brute he expected, but a smiling, radiant man, for Ishii the murderer had been born again!

The Bible *informs*, *reforms* and *transforms*.
It "informs" in that it tells us of Jesus.
It "reforms" in that it helps to "make all things new" in us.
It "transforms" because it teaches us about the power and grace of God.

Information, reformation, transformation.
The Bible has them all.

Read St. Luke 23: 26–34.

MONTH FOUR

Nothing great is done easily!

Sometimes people speak of "inspiration" as if it involved no effort. You sit down and write and, hey presto, it happens! The evidence is all against that point of view.

Lord Byron and Lord Tennyson were two of the great masters of verse-making. But we are told both used rhyming dictionaries!

Their rhyming words seem to us to come with a complete inevitability, falling into place naturally and effortlessly. But time and time again they were the result of laboriously studying a dictionary to find a word which would rhyme.

You might think that a lyric poet above all would sing as a bird sings, with no effort and with instinctive ease! But W. B. Yeats, the great Irish poet, tells of his debt to Lady Gregory in a time of weakness after an illness: "I asked her to send me to work every day at eleven, and at some other hour to my letters, rating me with idleness, if need be, and I doubt if I could have done much with my life but for her firmness and her care."

It may seem odd to think of a lyric poet being sent to his desk, at eleven a.m., but that was the way in which the poet's work was done.

Balzac, the master of the short story, speaks of himself as "plying the pick for dear life like an entombed miner". Not much sound of effortless ease there.

Flaubert, the master of French style, speaks of himself as "sick, irritated, the prey a thousand times a day of cruel pain," yet "continuing my labour like a true working-man, who, with sleeves turned up, in the sweat of his brow, beats away at his anvil, whether it rain or blow, hail or thunder."

It is hard work that produces that which is great.
There is no easier way!

Read Nehemiah 4: 1–6.

Per ardua ad astra runs the motto of the Royal Air Force. We reach the stars, the heights, through hard ways.

Yes, the way to the stars is steep!

A man came to James Agate, who in his lifetime was probably the most distinguished of all dramatic critics, and asked him for the secret of how to become a drama critic. James Agate's reply was that he must study the works of about thirty great dramatists to see what great drama is, before he dared to become a critic at all. The man objected that he would be at least forty before he had got through the list. Agate's reply was, "You must be at least forty before your opinions have any value."

It is through sweat, tears and toil that we achieve greatness.

There is no other way.

We hear a lot today about more pay for shorter hours. But leisure and luxury can only be safely secured through sacrifice.

"The Kingdom of Heaven" said the famous Christian writer, James Denney, "is not for the well-meaning but for the desperate."

To go uphill means effort.

To despise effort invites decline.

Yes, the way to the stars is steep!

Read St. Matthew 26: 36–46.

FROM TRAGEDY TO TRIUMPH   Day Three

One of the great missionary stories is the story of Mary Reed. In India she was haunted and oppressed by the fate of the lepers, for in those days nothing was done for them.

She herself took ill with an illness which no one could

diagnose. A visit to a hill station made no difference. She was sent home, and still no one could place her trouble. She had a numbness in one of her fingers and a stubbornly unhealable spot on her face.

At last a doctor realised what was the matter with her. She had contracted leprosy herself.

She was told the news. What was her reaction? Her reaction was to go down on her knees and to thank God that he had made her a leper, for she loved the lepers.

Mary Reed went back to India and for many years, herself a leper, worked among the lepers and was the means of bringing health and hope to them.

"All things work together for good to them that love God," says St. Paul (Rom. 8: 28).

Mary Reed thanked God for a disaster, because it brought a marvellous opportunity.

Tragedy can become, in God's hands, a triumph.

The Cross became resurrection.

Read Philippians 2: 5–11.

EXTERNALS   Day Four

It is risky to judge a book solely by its cover.

It is similarly dangerous to judge people by their physical appearance.

The truly great can look insignificant.

William Wilberforce, who was responsible for the freeing of the slaves throughout the British Empire, was weak in health, insignificantly small in body, and without any external attractions.

Boswell heard him speak, and said, "I saw what seemed to be a shrimp mount upon the table; but, as I listened, he grew until the shrimp became a whale."

Don't judge people by "externals".

It is the same when we make judgments of the Church. A

stately building, a noble liturgy, a large congregation can be important "externals". But they do not make the Church what it ought to be. For it is the quality of the people who are the Church that is vital.

Jesus puts "externals" in their perspective in the Sermon on the Mount.

It is not enough, he says, not to murder; we must never even feel anger in the heart. It is not enough not to commit adultery; the unclean desire must never even enter our heart. This is the test by which we are all judged and by which we all fail.

Few of us have hit a fellow-man; but what Jesus says is that we must never even have the wish to strike.

Few of us have committed adultery; but Jesus says that no unclean desire must ever enter the heart.

It is not the "externals" that matter in the end.
It is what is in the heart.

Read St. Matthew 15: 10–20.

THE LONG VIEW   Day Five

Lord Northcliffe was gifted with very long sight. It was said of him that he could read the prices of articles in shop windows while he was sitting in a taxi-cab driving down the middle of the road. But by far the most of his time was spent reading books and newspapers.

At one time he was threatened with blindness. A London oculist took the view that only an operation could save Northcliffe's sight. Northcliffe was unwilling to undergo an operation, and instead went to a German eye specialist. His verdict was that Northcliffe was suffering from extreme weariness of the optic nerve. And the cure was that Northcliffe must at least for a time give up looking at things close at hand, and only look at things in the distance and far away.

There is a lot of sense in taking "a long view" in life.

This applies to things we are tempted to do. It doesn't seem likely that they will affect us badly at that moment, but sometimes present actions lead on to things that will damage.

"Think before you act" is a good maxim.

It can save long-term unhappiness.

Anthony Collett was building a country cottage and planning to lay out the garden of it. In charge of operations in the garden there was an old man. Anthony Collett had given him instructions to plant apple trees and walnut trees in certain places. But the old man came to him and said, "You did tell me to plant apple trees there; but I have put the walnut trees here, and the apple trees there, for I did think that when you and me were gone, those walnuts would shade them apples."

To think ahead has advantages.

Read James 5: 7–8.

THINK BEFORE YOU ACT!   Day Six

A certain American sociologist made an examination of the descendants of a drunken man whom he called Martin Kalikak and who married a woman as bad as himself.

This investigation was made in 1920; Martin Kalikak lived about 1770.

In the intervening 150 years, Martin Kalikak's descendants had totalled 480. Of these, 143 were feeble-minded; thirty-six were illegitimate; twenty-four were alcoholics; three were epileptics; eighty-two died in infancy; and three were executed for capital crimes.

What a lot of evil came from two people who individually and together were of poor quality.

What we do today can bring trouble to us—and to the world—tomorrow.

Equally it can bring blessing.

Yes. "Think before you act."

Read James 3: 13–18.

It is very easy to "label" people.

Some people fall into the mistake of putting people in "pigeon-holes". It is all too easy to do this and in doing it to reduce people to being just objects.

Clifford Bax writes of George Russell, or "A.E." as he was commonly called, "People were not real to A.E. Never once did he show any interest in a man's background, in his hopes, in his troubles. We were shadows, shadows and listeners."

George Russell was quite detached in his attitude to men; to him men were not persons with hearts and emotions and feelings and experiences; to him they were merely an audience to talk to and to impress.

H. G. Wells, who knew her well, said of Beatrice Webb, the famous Fabian socialist, "She saw men as samples moving." To her again people were not persons; they were samples and specimens to be statistically analysed and recorded and entered on schedules.

On the other hand, James Agate wrote of G. K. Chesterton, "Unlike some other thinkers, Chesterton understood his fellow-men; the woes of a jockey were as familiar to him as the worries of a judge ... Chesterton, more than any man I have ever known had the common touch. He would give the whole of his attention to a bootblack." Anybody, jockey, judge, bootblack, was to Chesterton a person in whom he was determined to identify himself.

If there is one thing on which the Christian faith exists, it is the importance of each and every one of us as individuals.

You are of more value than many sparrows, said Jesus.

People matter, old and young.

Read St. Matthew 19: 13–15.

John Woolman, the great American Quaker, was a man with an ever passionate desire to enter into the experience of others, so that he might be able to understand and, therefore, help them. He made a voyage across the Atlantic in the steerage of an uncomfortable little ship. The atmosphere of the dark, crowded space between the decks was often almost unbearably foul.

Woolman wrote: "Several nights of late I have felt my breathing difficult; and a little after the rising of the second watch which is about midnight, I have got up and stood near an hour with my face near the hatches to get fresh air ... But I was glad to experience what many thousands of my fellow-creatures often suffer in a greater degree."

This is what the word "identification" means.

To "identify" with someone means to share fully in their experiences.

The prophet Ezekiel has a wonderful phrase that expresses his desire to be "identified" with the people.

"I sat where they sat," he says, as we said before.

When we use the big word "incarnation" of Jesus' coming into the world, we are saying just the same sort of thing about God. "God was *in* Christ, reconciling the world to Himself," Paul says. God became "incarnate" in Jesus. Or to put it very literally God "took on flesh" in Jesus in order that he might "identify" with us. In fact one of the loveliest names given to Jesus was that of "Immanuel". And that word simply means "God with us".

Identification truly!

So St. John says "the Word was made flesh and dwelt among us."

Or to use big words: the Incarnation is God's "identification" with his people.

Read Ezekiel 3: 4–15.

101

Are you a nuisance?

If you are, you won't be very popular!

But some of the men who have done most for the world really have been nuisances to it.

Socrates was called "the gadfly" because he stung men out of their contented, sleepy lethargies.

Antisthenes, the great Cynic philosopher, used to say that truth is like the light to sore eyes, and he who never hurts anyone, never helps anyone either.

A man from Corinth once said of the Athenians, who were the explorers of the world and of the mind, "You Athenians never rest yourselves, and you will never let anyone else rest either."

Jesus likened the Kingdom of God to leaven, and when leaven is put into the dough, it makes the dough bubble and seethe and erupt (Matt. 13: 33).

The Thessalonians characterised the Christians as those who were turning the world upside down (Acts 17: 6).

Two men were once talking about a great satirist who bravely and passionately rebuked the world for its sins and follies and mistakes. "He kicked the world about", said one, "as if it had been his football." "True," said the other, "but he kicked it to the goal."

"You are a 'trouble' to Israel," they told Elijah. But he was simply being God's nuisance.

If you are really going to do something valuable in the world, you may have to be a nuisance.

Read 1 Kings 18: 17–20.

CRUCIFY HIM?   **Day Ten**

What would happen, if Jesus came again? Suppose

Jesus were to be born into our town and our community today, what would happen to him?

Might he not be crucified again?

There is a famous story of an almost savage saying of Thomas Carlyle.

One evening he was at a small literary gathering. There was present a gushing, sentimental lady who was inveighing against the Jews for what they had done to Jesus. She insisted on how terrible and how wicked these people had been. She was so sorry, she said, that Jesus had not appeared in her time, for she at least would have delighted to honour him and to welcome him. "How delighted," she said, "we would have been to throw open our doors to him, and to listen to his divine precepts. Don't you think so, Mr. Carlyle?"

Carlyle answered, "No, Madam, I don't. I think that, had he come fashionably dressed with plenty of money and preaching doctrines palatable to the higher orders, I might have had the honour of receiving from you a card of invitation on the back of which would be written 'To meet our Saviour'. But, if he had come uttering his sublime precepts, and denouncing the Pharisees, and associating with publicans and the lower orders, as he did, you would have treated him much as the Jews did, and have cried out 'Take him to Newgate and hang him'."

True?

Jesus spoke the Truth.
He would do it again.
There are many who would not like him for that today, just as they hated it long ago.

Read Hebrews 6: 1–6.

NO ROOM   Day Eleven

There was no room for Jesus in the inn.

103

A certain artist, Sigismund Goetze, had a picture hung in the Royal Academy of 1904, entitled "Despised and Rejected of Men". He showed Christ on the steps of St. Paul's Cathedral, with the passing crowd blind to his presence.

One man almost brushes against him as he passes, buried in his sporting newspaper.

A scientist is too busy with his test-tube to see Christ.

A couple bent on pleasure hurry into a taxi with never a look at him.

A dignitary of the Church, sleek, self-satisfied, with an air of piety, passes by oblivious of Christ.

A non-conformist parson passes by so engaged in theological arguments and polemics that he does not even see him.

A mob orator harangues the crowd on the rights of men, with never a look for the great Brother of all men.

Only a nurse glimpses Christ and passes on.

We said yesterday that if Jesus came again, he would be crucified.

The other possibility is that people wouldn't bother. They "couldn't care less"—and would just ignore him.

"He came unto his own and his own received him not".

It is a sad commentary on the ability of people to recognise real goodness.

But some would welcome him, I'm sure.

Would you be among them?

Read 1 John 1: 1–10

EXPECT A LOT! Day Twelve

One of the great characteristic facts of life is that, by and large, we make men what we expect them to be. If we treat a man as if we expected him to be an unpleasant character, he will very likely be an unpleasant character; and if we treat a man as if we expected him to act like a man of honour, we will probably find him a man of honour.

Suspicion begets suspicion; and a low view of man produces low men.

It is those who expect the best from men who get the best from men. A schoolboy said of Thomas Arnold, the great headmaster of Rugby, "A fellow can't tell Arnold a lie, because he always believes what you say."

Arnold's belief in the honour of his boys laid an obligation of honour on the boys.

One of the most famous character sketches ever written was the sketch of a beloved captain written by Donald Hankey in the 1914–18 war.

The captain came to the platoon; he picked out the awkward ones, not to bully and to criticise them, but to help them. He clearly believed that they could become good soldiers. "His confidence was infectious. He looked at them, and they looked at him, and the men pulled themselves together and determined to do their best. Their best surprised themselves."

Men talked about his smile. "It meant something. It meant that we were his men, and he was proud of us, and sure that we were going to do jolly well—better than any other of the platoons. And it made us determined that we would."

What a marvellous character sketch that was!

Jesus expected a lot from his disciples.
They gave a lot.

Will you?

Read St. Luke 17: 5–10.

AMAZING VALUE   Day Thirteen

I remember going to work on Bible translation in Oxford

without a very essential part of my luggage. I went without an English Bible!

So I went into the town to get a Bible, and very naturally, since I am well equipped with Bibles at home, I did not want to buy an expensive one.

Then I happened on what must be very nearly the Bible bargain of all time—the Fontana edition of the Revised Standard Version, magnificently printed and, even in its paper covers, beautifully bound, and all for some forty pence. I had not known that this edition existed until I saw it then; and it seemed to be the cheapest price for the "best book" that I had ever seen.

How fortunate we are! In the early days, books were copied by hand. There was, in the fourth century A.D., when the great manuscripts were being copied, a standard rate of pay for scribes.

Books for copying were divided into what were called stichoi. A stichos (the singular form of the word) is not a line. It was originally the length of certain types of poetry—the line in which Homer wrote—and it counted as sixteen syllables. So books were classed as having so many stichoi, and, of course, however you recopied them and arranged them on the page, the number of stichoi remained constant.

Now there is a sixth-century New Testament manuscript called the "Codex Claromontanus" which gives the number of stichoi in each New Testament book. Further, there is an edict of Diocletian published early in the fourth century which fixes the prices for all sorts of things; and amongst other things it fixes the rates for the pay of scribes; and the pay is twenty to twenty-five denarii per hundred stichoi. A denarius was about four pence; so we may say that the rate was approximately one hundred pence per hundred stichoi.

Now in Matthew there are 2,600 stichoi, in Mark 1,600, in Luke 2,900 and in John 2,000. So in the four Gospels there are 9,100 stichoi. At that time a copy of the four Gospels would cost ninety-one pounds. If you work it out on the same basis, a copy of the letters of Paul would cost more than fifty pounds!

And now you can buy the whole Bible for less than fifty pence!

It's amazing value!

Read St. Luke 4: 16–21.

NO EXCUSE   Day Fourteen

When Wycliffe published the Bible in English for the first time at the end of the fourteenth century, it was, of course, before printing was invented. The Bible still had to be copied by hand.

Later, George Foxe was to say, "Some gave five marks (equal to about forty pounds in modern money), some more, some less for a book. Some gave a load of hay for a few chapters of St. James or St. Paul in English."

Think of the price at which *we* can buy the word of God.

When the Great Bible was published in 1540, Bishop Bonner placed the six copies in convenient places in St. Paul's Cathedral; and such was the eagerness to read them, and to hear them read aloud, that services were rendered impossible and the traffic disrupted and the crowds so great that Bonner had to threaten to take the Bibles away if the eager disorder did not cease.

What a difference today!

When Bibles are as easy to get as is the case today, we have no excuse for not having one, have we?

Read Psalm 33: 1–11.

RIGHTS AND DUTIES   Day Fifteen

There are certain things that stand out in the life of Albert Schweitzer.

One is this.

He did not say: "What does the world owe me?", but "What do I owe the world?"

By the time he was thirty, three worlds lay open to Albert Schweitzer for the conquering; and it was then that he embarked upon a course of six years of medical training which was to be the prelude to his life-work in his hospital in Lambarene.

By that time he was a Doctor of Philosophy, and a brilliant academic career was his for the taking. He had studied the organ under Charles Marie Widor in Paris, and, young as he was, he was the foremost authority on the music of Bach.

By that time he was a Doctor of Theology and was already Principal of the Theological College at Strasbourg, with an attractive house, a good stipend, and the prospect of an honourable and brilliant career as a theological teacher and thinker.

It was then that he took the road that ended in Lambarene.

It was not a sudden decision. It was a decision that went back to a summer morning, full of happiness and beauty, at Gunsbach nine years before. On that morning, as Schweitzer tells, "There came to me as I awoke the thought that I must not accept this happiness as a matter of course, but must give something in return for it."

Many people today insist on their *rights*, what is *due* to them, what they ought to *get* from society. But often people forget their *duties*, that is what they ought to *give* to society.

"Whosoever shall seek to save his life shall lose it" said Jesus. But "Whosoever is willing for my sake to lose his life shall find it."

"It is more blessed to give than to receive."

Schweitzer found all these sayings from the Bible are true.

Read Acts 20: 32–35.

108

Professor J. E. McFadyen learned Italian while travelling daily by train to his College in Glasgow. The journey took about half-an-hour each way. He used those half-hours to learn a new language!

We sometimes say "It's not worth starting." But these are dangerous words.

I remember finding myself behind with my work one day. I had to go out to an engagement. I had half-an-hour before I needed to leave my desk, and I had a definite job which ought to have been done. But I found myself saying "I've only got half-an-hour; it's not worth starting."

Often we find ourselves with a small amount of time. We know that there is something which ought to be done; and we say, "It's not worth beginning with so little time available."

It is a dangerous phrase. It means that the half-an-hour is wasted—and wasted half-hours soon mount up to a considerable amount of time. If we work a five-day week and waste half-an-hour each day, that is two and a half hours. Over a year that is one hundred and thirty hours; and one hundred and thirty hours is not much short of a week—a whole week's time and work wasted and gone.

Robert Louis Stevenson was a sick man and he knew that he had not very long to live. Sometimes he used to say: "If you can't finish your folio, at least get started on your page."

A lot can be done in half-an-hour.
It's *always* worth starting.

Read Psalm 90: 1–12.

THE BIBLE UP-TO-DATE   Day Seventeen

There has never been such a flood of new translations of

the New Testament as there has been in the past generation. The number of these new translations may have puzzled you.

You may ask, "Why new translations at all? Why can't we rest content with the Authorised Version?"

And there are some people for whom the Authorised Version is "the Bible" and who come near to resenting any attempt to change it; and some who would rather have its familiar cadences than any of the new translations.

Why then are the new translations necessary?
There is more than one answer to that question.

The Authorised Version emerged in 1611. The basis of the Greek text from which its translation was made was the text of Erasmus, whose first edition was published in 1516.

Now obviously, the older a Greek manuscript of the New Testament is, the more likely it is to be correct, because every time a manuscript was copied, new errors crept in. The nearer a manuscript is to the original writing, the less chance there is for error, and the more likely it is to be accurate.

The Greek text is the one from which the Authorised Version was made. No manuscript was known earlier than the twelfth century.

As the years went on, far older manuscripts were discovered. In the nineteenth century, Tischendorf discovered "Codex Sinaiticus", and "Codex Vaticanus" became available, and both of these manuscripts date back to the fourth century. In the present century, in 1931 the Chester Beatty manuscripts were discovered and they date back in some cases to the early part of the third century. As recently as 1958, the Bodmer manuscripts were discovered and they date as far back as A.D. 200 or thereby.

This means that we now possess manuscripts of the New Testament which are one thousand years older than anything from which the Authorised Version was made, one thousand years nearer the originals, and which are therefore very much more accurate.

The materials which we now possess from which to make a

translation are incomparably superior to anything that was available when the Authorised Version was produced.

Read Psalm 119: 97–104.

NEW KNOWLEDGE   Day Eighteen

The language of the Authorised Version is the language of 1611. It is therefore archaic. So we need new translations. Here are some examples to show why.

In Acts 28: 13 the Authorised Version has: "From thence we fetched a compass, and came to Rhegium." The phrase "fetched a compass" is now quite out of date. The Revised Standard Version has: "From there we made a circuit," and the New English Bible "we sailed round".

Acts 21: 15 is even more misleading in the Authorised Version: "After those days we took up our carriages, and went up to Jerusalem." Here "carriages" is used in the sense of "that which we had to carry". The New English Bible correctly has: "At the end of our stay we packed our baggage and took the road up to Jerusalem."

When the New Testament was first written in the original Greek, it spoke to men in the ordinary everyday language that they used daily. The English of 1611 cannot be like that to us. The Bible ought to speak to men in their own contemporary language; that is the way it originally spoke; and only a modern translation can make it so speak again.

We now know much more about the kind of language people spoke in New Testament times than the Authorised Version translators could have known. A host of documents has been discovered such as private letters, accounts, legal documents, income tax returns, census papers and minutes of meetings.

So today we have aids to the translation of the New Testament which did not exist in 1611; and to refuse to use them is to despoil ourselves of a new knowledge which can make the Bible more meaningful than ever.

Read Psalm 119: 105–112.

Listen to these words from Paul:

"I'm not ashamed of the Gospel of Christ" he said (Rom. 1: 16).

Are you?

Would you like to be seen saying grace in a café?

I remember hearing a lovely story about a family out for a meal together. After they had eaten, mother said: "Wasn't that lovely? I think we should say a grace to say thanks for it." "Why," said six-year-old Tommy, "we're paying for it."

Tommy's reason for questioning grace was a very practical one! But if you believe in saying grace at home, would you mind doing it in public?

There may be many situations later in life when you have to "stand up and be counted" for your faith, in public.

Will Paul's words be yours?

"Be not *con*formed to this world" says the Bible, "but be ye *trans*formed."

To be a non-conformist may be something you will have to do—for God's sake.

Read Romans 12: 1–5.

TRAVELLING ON   **Day Twenty**

Here are three very important questions:
Where do I come from?
Where am I going?
How do I get there?

Where do I come from?

Dr. H. E. Fosdick, the noted American preacher, once gave the "chemical" analysis of a man. "In a man there is enough fat to make seven bars of soap; enough iron to make a medium-sized nail; enough lime to whitewash a henhouse;

enough sugar to fill a sugar-sifter; enough magnesium for a dose of magnesia; enough potassium to explode a toy cannon: enough phosphorus to tip 2,200 matches; and a very little sulphur."

That is one answer to the question!

But Christians want to say more than this. They say that all life, including human life, comes from *God*. It is not a collection of chemical elements. It is not a chance conglomeration. It is a gift of God.

Do you agree?

Where am I going?

If life is a gift from God, it is then something to give back to God.

Some people would say we are going *nowhere*. Death is the end and there is nothing beyond it. We are simply obliterated, and there is no more to be said.

Our faith is different from this. It believes that what we are and do in life matters because death is not the end. It is rather the gateway to a greater, truer life.

So we are, as Sydney Carter says, "travelling on".

How do we get there?

The Christian faith gives a simple answer:
"I am the Way," said Jesus.

Christians believe he is.
That is how we get there.

Read St. John 14: 1–7.

DETOURS   Day Twenty-one

London taxi-drivers, I have been told, have to pass a very strict police examination to make sure that they know the shortest way between any two points in the city.

One candidate had studied the maps until he knew them by heart. In the examination he was asked the quickest way from one place to another. He gave it according to the map.

He was failed, because the route he indicated was the quickest all right, but it would have involved driving the taxi down a lengthy flight of steps and through a lane too narrow for a bicycle!

Sometimes we need to take detours.
The quickest way may not be the right way.

If you are going to be a "leader" you will find this is true.
Some people can move fast—others can't. So patience has to be shown if, as the leader, you are going to get support from everyone in your group or team.

The same is true in trying to introduce something new. People don't like changes! So you will find getting new things accepted is very hard.
You have to take a detour. It will mean the patient sowing of an idea in people's minds and then just waiting for it to take root and become accepted.
When it is accepted, it may well be presented as their new idea when it was really yours. But who owns the idea does not matter! The important thing is that it is accepted.

Jesus once took a detour. He went on his journey, but deliberately not through Samaria. He had a good reason for the detour and it was worth it.
Don't be afraid of detours.
They are often justified in the end!

Read St. Luke 17: 11–19.

HISTORY   Day Twenty-two

"History is bunk," said Henry Ford, the American car magnate.
"I would have him learn a little history," said Oliver Cromwell.

Here are two views on history!
Which is right?

Both are right.
Why?
Because history has its uses *and* abuses.

History can lead to *pessimism*.
We sometimes say, sadly, that you can't change human
nature. We still have wars, corruptions, profiteering, vic-
timisation, and so on. So we say: "You will never get rid
of these things, because you just can't change human
nature."

But, on the other hand, a missionary tells how he pre-
sided over a communion service in central Africa. At that
communion service the members of two African tribes sat
in perfect love and harmony. Less than a generation
before it had been the custom for the young warriors of
these tribes, as they came to manhood, to go out to wet
their spears in each other's blood, to steal each other's
women, to burn each other's houses, and to destroy each
other's crops. They had done it for centuries. It was en-
graved into tribal ritual and custom—and yet the power of
Jesus Christ had brought ancestral enemies together in
fellowship around the table of love.

History can teach both hope and despair.
The Christian belief however is that there is always
hope when Christ is taken into account.

Read Psalm 1.

DECISIONS Day Twenty-three

Do you ever delay decisions by saying "I'll think about
it"?
I suspect it means we don't really want to make a decision
at all!

There is a famous story of how, in a moment of crisis in the history of Greece, Agesilaus, the Spartan king, assembled his men and prepared to go into action. He sent word to another of the Greek rulers asking him to come to help in the hour of their country's peril. The other king replied that he would consider it. Agesilaus sent back the answer: "Tell him that while he is considering it, we will march."

When we want to "think about it", we must be careful we are not simply avoiding the question.

"I'll think about it" may mean two other things.

It can mean that we believe that if we think about a problem, it will solve itself!

Sometimes thinking *must* become *doing*. It is as simple as that.

The other danger in "thinking about it" is simply that we miss the boat by doing that!

Someone needs help. What do we do?

We think about it.

It is too late. The moment of need has gone.

Thinking is a good and necessary exercise. Not to think about things is quite wrong. But don't let us make thinking an end in itself. It is a means that should lead to action.

Let us be sure we do reach the action!

Read Matthew 25: 1–13.

BACK ROOM BOYS   Day Twenty-four

Timothy, of all his helpers, was closest to St. Paul.

"I have no one like him" said St. Paul (Phil. 2: 20).

He calls him his beloved and faithful child (1 Cor. 4: 17; 1 Tim. 1: 2; 2 Tim. 1: 2).

To St. Paul, Timothy was like a son.

It was at the beginning of the second missionary journey

116

that St. Paul took Timothy on to his staff. Timothy's mother's name was Eunice (2 Tim. 1: 5).

It is in the Acts 16: 1–4 that we read the first meeting of Timothy with St. Paul.

Now from that passage there is every reason to believe that Eunice was a widow. There are Latin manuscripts which in the first verse call the mother of Timothy *vidua*, and there are certain Greek manuscripts which call her *chera*, and both words mean widow. And it may be in verse three that we could translate, "For they all knew that his father had been a Greek."

Now, if Eunice was a widow, and if Timothy was her only son, and beyond doubt a good son too, it must have been not only a wrench but a very considerable sacrifice to see her son go off adventuring with Paul for Jesus Christ. Surely the home of Eunice must have been an emptier and financially much poorer place without the young Timothy there.

In the background of Timothy there probably stands a mother, Eunice, of whom the Church at large has never really heard, but to whom the Church owed Timothy.

There are in life very many to this day who are still described in terms of someone else. They are known as someone's husband, someone's wife, someone's brother, someone's sister, someone's son. For the most part they never complain and they never grudge the limelight or the leading place to their more famous friend, relation, or partner. They are content, and well content to take second place.

We need leaders, but we need back room boys like Timothy.

And we should remember gratefully, even further in the background, those who are prepared to let a dear one go.

I have a great admiration for those who happily take second place.

Read 2 Timothy 1: 1–5.

I don't like stories about toothache! But here is one that teaches us something.

A man was sitting in his garden suffering agonies with toothache, trying to make up his mind to visit the dentist.

He thought that he would have a cup of tea and a piece of bread and jam. He got the tea and the bread and jam; he took a bite of the bread and jam without noticing that a wasp had settled on it. When he took the bite, the wasp stung him extremely painfully in the gum. He dashed indoors and saw in the mirror that the gum was swollen and inflamed; he treated it and bathed it and gradually the pain subsided; he suddenly realised that the pain of the toothache was gone too.

A doctor, hearing this story, said it could happen! One pain may actually cancel out another. In other words, the best way to get rid of one pain is to have another!

When a farmer looks at a weedy piece of ground, he tears out the weeds; but he does not then leave the ground empty; he displaces the weeds with a useful crop.

In life the way to get rid of a bad thing is to displace it with a good thing. This is a lesson of the parable of the empty house (Luke 11: 24–26). The demon was ejected from the house; the house was swept clean; but it was left empty; and the consequence was that the demon came back with seven demons worse than himself and reoccupied the empty house. To keep the demon out, he should have been displaced by good occupants.

The best principle in life is that of displacement.
It is a much better solution than emptiness.

Read St. Luke 11: 17–26.

Let's look further at this "principle of displacement".

You won't get rid of evil and unclean thoughts just by saying, "I will not think of this or that". To do that usually means concentrating thoughts on the very thing you don't want to think! You need *new* thoughts, *good* thoughts, *new* interests, *good* interests. It's not a question of just emptying your mind of the bad. Put in the good!

You won't get rid of a disappointment by just trying to forget it. You need to replace it with *hope*.

The psychologists use a big word, "sublimation", to help people sadly disappointed. All the energy we should have given to the situation we have lost must go to somewhere else.

We mustn't leave holes!

We must fill them!

It is the same with sadness and sorrow.

The best way to forget sorrow is to enter someone else's sorrow. To think only of your own sadness is to ensure continued sorrow and even resentment. To lose yourself in others' sorrow will do far more good.

There really is something in this principle of displacement!

Read Psalm 51: 1–13.

THE MEANING OF RELIGION   Day Twenty-seven

I remember looking at a certain newspaper on the night President John Kennedy of the United States died by assassination.

Usually that particular paper gives a certain amount of space to religion. It was usually one page. That night that page was missing!

That doesn't sound very important. But here is the point. In that issue five columns were given to racing, five to news of the entertainment world, a whole page to women's topics and a short story. There were even included the usual horoscopes and "what the stars foretell".

I know enough about journalism and the way papers are put together to know that the Church page "copy" was probably ready in advance, and might even have been unsuitable in the new circumstances. But I also know enough about journalism to realise that any fast-working journalist could have re-written the copy and given a Church view on that awful news.

But nobody thought it worthwhile: what the Church might have to say does not matter.

But isn't this what is reflected in the *personal* religion of so many people today. If as Paul says "Christ means *life* to me" (Phil. 1: 21) then the place religion has in our lives will be important to us and it will get priority.

Lord Melbourne said long ago, "Religion is all right so long as it does not interfere with a man's private life." This is nonsense, for it denies the meaning of religion!

Read Romans 14: 13–17.

IF YOURS WERE THE ONLY JOB . . .

Day Twenty-eight

A well-known bacteriologist told me about a little assistant that he had.

About 300 samples of milk had come into his laboratory for testing; and it was the assistant who had to do the testing. He was sorry for her faced with such a task; so he said, "Isn't that far too much for you to do?" "Oh no," she said, "I'll just do them one at a time!"

There is a Chinese saying that tells the same truth; "A journey of a thousand miles begins with one single step."

This is excellent advice if you have a lot of work to do or a big job to undertake.

In anything big like this, the first step is (strange as it seems) to make a start! It is as simple as that.

When you are faced with a lot of work, it is so easy to sit and look at it and never actually begin. So whether it is washing dishes, writing a letter, paying a visit, working for an exam, *take that step!*

And here is another bit of advice! The only way to get a job done is to attack it as if it was the only job in the world.

Put your heart into it!

Making a start, taking the first step, is often an act of faith. Have that faith! Make an act of faith.

Abraham went out, not knowing where he was going.

But he went.

That's what mattered.

That's what was important for the purposes of God.

Read Hebrews 11: 8–14.

KEEP GOING!   Day Twenty-nine

You remember the old fable by Aesop about the hare and the tortoise?

A hare one day ridiculed the short feet and slow pace of the tortoise. The latter, laughing, said, "Though you be swift as the wind I will beat you in a race." The hare, thinking his assertion to be simply impossible, agreed to the proposal; and they decided that the fox should choose the course, and fix the goal.

On the day appointed for the race they started together. The tortoise never for a moment stopped, but went on with a slow but steady pace straight to the end of the course. The hare, trusting to his native swiftness, cared little about the race, and lying down by the wayside, fell fast asleep.

At last waking up, and moving as fast as he could, he saw that the tortoise had reached the goal, and was comfortably dozing with fatigue.

"The race is not to the swift, nor the battle to the strong," said the Preacher (Eccles. 9: 11).

Perseverance counts in the end.

Get started!
Keep going!
You will get there!

Read Hebrews 11: 32–12: 12.

ONE SOLITARY LIFE   Day Thirty

I would like to give you a marvellous description of Jesus. I saw it on a Y.M.C.A. notice-board. You may have seen it somewhere else.

It is taken from a newspaper printed in Ontario but who wrote it is not known.

It is called "One Solitary Life".

I like it and I hope you will.

Here is a man who was born of Jewish parents in an obscure village, the child of a peasant woman. He grew up in another obscure village. He worked in a carpenter's shop until he was thirty, and then, for three years, he was an itinerant preacher.

He never wrote a book, he never held an office, he never owned a home. He never had a family. He never went to college. He never put his foot inside a big city. He never travelled two hundred miles from the place where he was born. He never did one of these things that usually accompany greatness. He had no credentials but himself.

He had nothing to do with this world, except the naked power of his manhood. While still a young man the tide of popular opinion turned against him. His friends ran away. One of them denied him. He was turned over to his enemies. He went through the mockery of a trial.

He was nailed to a cross, between two thieves. His executioners gambled for the only piece of property he had on earth, while he was dying—and that was his coat. When he was dead he was taken down and laid in a borrowed grave, through the pity of a friend.

Nineteen wide centuries have come and gone, and today he is the centre-piece of the human race, and the leader of the column of progress. I am far within the mark when I say that all the armies that ever marched, and all the navies that were ever built, and all the parliaments that ever sat, and all the kings that ever reigned, put together, have not affected the life of man upon earth as powerfully as has that solitary life.

Read Acts 13: 23–39.

IT IS ALWAYS EASTER   EASTER DAY

We seem to think of Easter only at Easter time—as if the Resurrection of Jesus only mattered then.

How wrong this is!

If we think like this, we must have forgotten the origin of Sunday, or the Lord's Day as we call it.

The Sabbath, the Jewish holy day, commemorated the rest from his labours God enjoyed after creating the earth.

Sunday marks the resurrection of Jesus.

Every week we should remember he rose from the dead.

If Jesus didn't rise from the dead, then, said Paul, "we are of all men most miserable". And he meant it. For he felt Jesus' resurrection was at the very centre of our faith.

Each Sunday marks that fact.

It is always Easter!

Read 1 Corinthians 15: 12–20.

123

MONTH FIVE

"The good eye, the humble mind, the lowly spirit."
Who should have these attributes?
A true son of Abraham, according to a Jewish saying.

The good eye? By this is meant not so much the good eye
physically, but the *generous* eye. A good man will look with
generosity on people.

We can be generous in various ways.
One way is by our encouragement.

There used to be a regulation in the Royal Navy which
stated that "no officer shall speak to any other officer
discouragingly in the performance of his duty."
To encourage generously is a good quality.

Another way is by our "sensitivity", that is our ability to
"feel" someone's need and respond to it. To sense deeply
and help quickly are marks of "the good eye".

Yet another way is by our forgiveness, our ability to over-
look a fault.

One of the most startling sentences in the Authorised
Version is the sentence which tells us that God "winked at
the former times of ignorance". God in his mercy, when
men did not know any better, turned a blind eye to their
faults and failings (Acts 17: 30).

Just as there is a gift in seeing, there is sometimes a gift
in not seeing. The wise man knows what to see and what
not to see.

There are times when the blind eye is as great a virtue as
the seeing eye.

A blind eye can strangely enough be an expression of the good eye.

Read Acts 17: 22–30.

THE RIGHT BALANCE

Do you ever feel nervous?
Here is one way to deal with nerves!

I once read an article by Andrew Wilson on lions and lion taming. Mr. Wilson relates a very interesting story.

One day, a young man called Bobby Ramsay turned up at his zoo asking for a job; he wanted, of all extraordinary things, to be taken on as a lion tamer. When asked why, his reason was still more extraordinary. He was in fact in serious danger of a nervous breakdown, and his doctor had told him that the only thing that would cure him would be to get so nerve-racking a job that he would forget the other fears which haunted him. So he applied for the most dangerous job he could think of, and he became a very well-known lion tamer. His nervous breakdown was cured.

The way to get rid of nerves was to tackle something that demanded nerve.

Now here is a suggestion as to how to lighten your own burden.

Help some one with his!

Teilhard de Chardin tells how on his expeditions in the wilder parts of China on horseback, the load would be hung on one side of the horse and on the other there was a stone to balance it. And it is well known that African carriers who carry loads on poles laid across their shoulders hang a stone on the other end of the pole as a counterbalance.

Two suitcases can sometimes be carried more easily than one.

They balance each other.

So do burdens—ours and his.

It is in the right balance that the answer to our sorrow lies!

Read Galatians 6: 1–5.

CRAMP Day Three

Do you ever get cramp?

It's a very unpleasant feeling. It happens when, as it were, a muscle knots.

Different people have different ways of dealing with cramp and very interesting some of them are.

Dr. Roger Bannister, the first man to run a mile in less than four minutes, claims to have beaten cramp by carrying a small magnet around with him.

A Hampshire housewife takes a bag of corks to bed with her to beat cramp.

A London man claims that barrel bungs are best.

Others use a ring of buffalo horn, a crimson thread tied round each toe, the powdered teeth of a sea-horse, the skin of an eel, a hippopotamus' tooth. All of them claim that their own special method brings a cure.

All this sound like the old days of spells and magic! What it does show is that if you think something is going to do you good, it will! Or to put it another way: the cure is in the mind, not the body.

This is, in a sense, what faith is like. If you believe something can be done, it will be done.

With God all things are possible, it says in Matthew 19: 26. Life therefore should have a strong element of faith in it. If you believe in your heart that something is possible, you are half-way to success.

If the mind believes, the body will certainly try to follow!

Read St. Matthew 19: 16–26.

There is in Khartoum a very famous statue of that great Christian soldier, General Gordon. It shows Gordon mounted on his horse.

One day a small boy was taken to see the statue and was told that it was a statue of Gordon. At the end of the day, his father said to him, "Well, you saw Gordon's statue today and that was something worth seeing and remembering." "Yes," said the small boy, "I liked seeing it very much. It's a lovely statue. But tell me, Dad, who is the man on Gordon's back?"

The horse was what really mattered to that boy! It wasn't the statue of a man on a horse. It was the statue of a horse with a man on it.

Sometimes we get our emphasis wrong. We let the unimportant overshadow the important.

Dag Hammarskjöld, the one time secretary of the United Nations, left behind him his diaries. Remarkable selections from them have been published under the title *Markings*. One extract tells us about a man who "was a member of the crew of Columbus' ship—he kept wondering whether he would get back to his home village in time to succeed the old shoemaker before anyone else could grab the job."

Here is the picture of a man who, when continents were being discovered, could not see beyond a job in the village shoemaker's shop; when he was involved in the greatest possible events, he could not see beyond his own tiny and petty concerns.

Jesus had something to say on right emphasis. He wanted us to get our priorities right.

"Seek ye first the Kingdom of God and his righteousness and all these things shall be added to you," are famous words we quoted before (Month One, Day Nineteen).

Have you got your priorities right?

Read Ecclesiastes 9: 13–18.

WHAT ARE *YOUR* AIMS? Day Five

Anyone who is interested in railways is bound to know the books of O.S. Nock. In his book *British Steam Railways,* he has a chapter about the early days when the railways were growing up, and when travel was still an adventure.

In it he tells how, more than a hundred years ago now, a little book of official advice to travellers was published entitled *Official Guide to the North Western Railway.* One section of this little Guide was entitled "Hints Before Starting".

The first three hints were as follows:

"Before commencing a journey the traveller should decide:
Whither he is going.
By what railway train and when.
Whether he will have to change carriages at any point, and where."

Then later on there is this: "The traveller is advised to take as little luggage as possible; and ladies are earnestly entreated not to indulge in more than seven boxes and five small parcels for the longest journey."

This is good sense for railway travellers! It is also good sense about life.

As you are setting out on the journey of life, then just *you* must decide where you are making for. If you do not know where you are going, you will (as they say colloquially) "get nowhere fast".

What is *your* aim to be?
To get—or to give?

131

To help one's fellow-men or to try to make the world do all it can for us?

To find a job satisfying or to think only of the money it brings?

To look for ways to serve people or work only at something which will ensure luxuries?

The great Dean Inge once said: "Bored people are those who are consuming much but producing little."

Do you want to be among those?

I don't think so.

Know where you are going.

Read Hebrews 13: 14–21.

TRAVEL LIGHT! Day Six

Let's think a bit more about hard work and effort!

The ancient writer, Hesiod, says that the gods have placed sweat as the price of all things. In other words, you only get success if you really work.

Some people think that success means finding the right people who will "have influence". They use other people just to help themselves on.

Using friends or acquaintances in this way is in itself wrong, for we are only using people as a means to an end (something God never does with us, incidentally). It is also non-productive, because in the end, it is not influence but effort that counts.

So when you set out on life, you must pick the right route —the road of effort and work.

In the Railway Guide we thought about yesterday, the advice was that we should not carry much luggage. This is true on life's journey too.

"A man's life," said Jesus, "does not consist in the abundance of his possessions" (Luke 12: 15).

We travel farthest and fastest if we travel light.
Happy travelling!

Read St. Matthew 10: 9–20.

TURN ROUND! Day Seven

Turn round!

You might not expect this to be said in the Bible. But in fact there is a lot in the Bible about "turning".

Here are some examples.

In Antioch a great number believed and *turned* to the Lord (Acts 11: 21).

Paul's task was to *turn* the Gentiles from darkness to light (Acts 26: 18).

The Thessalonians had *turned* to God from idols (1 Thess. 1: 9).

The promise of the Law is happiness and prosperity "if thou turn unto the Lord thy God with all thine heart and with all thy soul" (Deut. 30: 10).

The word "conversion" comes from the Latin word *convertere* and that of course means "to turn".

So conversion is the "turning-point" in our lives.

Turn round!

It is a good instruction.

It could be the most significant instruction in your life!

The turning-point in fact.

Read Psalm 80: 1–7.

THE TURNING POINT Day Eight

The word "conversion" (as we said yesterday) comes from the Latin word meaning "to turn". That is why our "conversion" is really the "turning-point" in our lives.

That "turning-point" may be a very dramatic one—as

Paul found when his turning-point began on the road to Damascus. And it is, too, for people who make decisions at a Billy Graham Crusade, for example. But it can also be the final point in a long process of growing certainty which will one day be expressed in taking your vows and becoming a member of "the Church".

There are three conversions—or turning points—in a man's life (George Ingle wrote in *The Lord's Creed*): the first is *to Christ;* the second is *to the Church;* and the third is "*back to the world*".
Let's just look at this.

The first step is to reach a firm belief (however it happens) in the wonder of Jesus and all he means: to realise he is "the Way, the Truth, and the Life".

The second step is to want to link up with people who share that conviction and express it in fellowship and service. "The Church" is that body of *people.*

The third step is to "go into all the world"—to want to go out in love to the world in Jesus' name.
These truly are great turning-points!

Read Acts 9: 1–9.

COMMITTED   Day Nine

Herbert Butterfield's words about facing the future are good advice: "Hold to Christ, and for the rest be totally uncommitted."
Any "conversion" which does not leave us totally committed to Jesus Christ is imperfect.

The shortest possible description of a Christian—a description with which the New Testament would fully agree—is that a Christian is a man who can say, "For me, Jesus Christ is Lord" (Rom. 10: 9; Phil. 2: 11).

134

The turning-point is real if it puts Jesus at the centre of our lives, thoughts, feelings, aims.

But here is a word of caution on the turning-point which is "conversion" and I would like you to think about it.

Conversion sometimes *separates* you from people when it should have the opposite effect. This may be because we become "self-righteous" as a result of what has happened to us; that is we may begin to think *we* are much better than our friends and then (like a Pharisee in the Bible) we become rather unpleasant people in every way.

The result of our reaching the turning-point we call "conversion" should be to make us humble, not overproud.

In other words, more like the publican, in the story Jesus told (Luke 18: 13).

Read Romans 10: 1–9.

OUR PEACE   Day Ten

There has never been a war between the Argentine and Chile, but in 1899 there was a frontier dispute which had highly explosive possibilities. By Easter 1900 the two armies were poised to strike and war seemed inevitable.

Monsignor Benavente preached in Buenos Aires, on Easter Day, a sermon which was a passionate appeal for peace. News of the sermon carried to Chile and a bishop in Chile took up the message. Both these bishops set out on a preaching campaign for peace.

At first little seemed to be happening and then bit by bit both nations were caught up in a great movement for peace.

In the end, the two governments were forced by the will of the people to submit the frontier dispute to the arbitration of King Edward VII of Britain.

A treaty was entered into which promised in future to submit all matters of dispute to arbitration. Then the wonderful thing happened. The guns of the frontier fortresses, now useless and irrelevant, were taken to the arsenal in Buenos

Aires and melted down. Out of them was cast a great bronze figure of Jesus.

The right hand is stretched out in blessing; the left holds a cross. It was decided to carry this great statue 13,000 feet up the mountains to the frontier. It was taken by train as far as the railway went; it was then taken on gun carriages drawn by mules; and for the final steep rise to the top of the mountain it was dragged up with ropes by soldiers and sailors. On March 13, 1904, it was at last erected and unveiled, and there it stands.

Beneath it are the words: "These mountains themselves shall fall and crumble to dust before the people of Chile and the Argentine Republic forget their solemn covenant sworn at the feet of Christ."

On the other side there is inscribed the text: "He is our peace who hath made both one." The text is Ephesians 2: 14.

That is surely a tale worth telling and worth remembering.

Read Ephesians 2: 8–22.

UPSIDE-DOWN!   Day Eleven

The ancient world was very divided. I don't mean in purely geographical terms, I am thinking of other more dangerous divisions.

There was the line drawn between Jew and Gentile. It made for bitterness.

There was a line between Greek and barbarian. It involved Greek contempt for his neighbour.

There was a hard line between slave and free man. The slave was little more than an object, a thing.

There was even a real line between male and female. The female had no legal rights at all.

Paul said: "There is neither Jew nor Greek, there is neither slave nor free, there is neither male nor female; for you are all one in Christ Jesus" (Gal. 3: 28).

136

See what Paul has done in that sentence. In the Jewish form of morning prayer, the Jew thanked God that "thou hast not made me a Gentile, a slave or a woman". Paul took that prayer, the prayer of his fathers, and once his own prayer, and turned it upside-down.

The lines are obliterated in these words!

The Christian Church has, unfortunately, sometimes fallen short of its ideals. It has been the "begetter", the "initiator", and the "blesser" of wars and violence. But it has had vast influence for good, too. It has broken down many "walls of division". It has been as it should be, "reconciling", exercising its "ministry of reconciliation".

Look again at that story of the statue on the Andes we thought about yesterday. It wasn't government-decided. It rose from the feelings of the people. *That* made their governments *do* something!

Read 2 Corinthians 5: 18–21.

POLITICS   Day Twelve

Dag Hammarskjöld, the former Secretary-General of the United Nations, wrote in *Markings*: "In our age the road to holiness necessarily passes through the world of action."

Here is an interesting but also a profound quotation from Charles Peguy. He says: "Everything begins in mysticism and ends in politics."

That says in a specific sense just what Dag Hammarskjöld means in a general sense.

Because of this, Christians—old and young—must find themselves involved in politics.

In a General Election some years ago, the election campaign at Smethwick in the Midlands of England was fought on the question of race and racial feelings.

Some people in Smethwick, who were connected with local government and also with the campaign, registered their objections to the fact that a Church of England vicar and certain of his fellow clergymen stated their mind on this matter. A member of a certain church is reported to have said: "I want an assurance from him that he will tackle preaching the Gospel and leave politics to us."

If we are Christians, we just can't take this attitude. We are not just concerned for the "spiritual" lives of people. We have to worry about their bodies. So social justice is our concern just because we are Christians.

We can't just forget that starving child in India.

We can't be unaware of the things bad housing does to people.

We must think about old people and what they need—in help, health, friendship.

We must be concerned about the sin of racial prejudice.

All this will involve us in politics, because that is what politics are about!

We really have no choice!

Read Isaiah 5: 8–10; 18–25.

FRIENDSHIP   Day Thirteen

"A friend is someone who knows all about you and still likes you."

That was the definition one schoolboy gave of friendship. I like it.

Friendship involves seeing people as they are, seeing them without (as we say) our "rose-coloured spectacles" on. True friendship must be based on real acceptance of each other.

"Fellowship" is another word of the same kind. It is a group of us getting together.

John Wesley said: "Is your heart as my heart? Then give me your hand!"

This is fellowship.

How does fellowship help us to live with others' faults? It does this by our being involved together in joint action and activity.

Yet the churches themselves are so divided still. How sad this is!

If you had escaped from a shipwreck in a small boat in the middle of a storm, you certainly would not ask if the man beside you was a Baptist, or a Methodist, or a Roman Catholic, or an Anglican before you joined him at an oar!

If you had to deal with a raging fire in a house, you quite certainly would not stop to ask to what branch of the Christian Church a man belonged, before you joined him, or allowed him to join you, in an attempt to extinguish the flames or to rescue those trapped in the house!

There is so much to do in the world in Jesus' name. All who follow him should *do* it together.

And in the doing of it the meaning of fellowship will be found.

Read 1 Samuel: 20: 35–42.

CLOSER THAN A BROTHER   Day Fourteen

There are friends who pretend to be friends.
But there is a friend who sticks closer than a brother.

The writer of the Proverbs said that.
How true it is.

C. F. Andrews used to have a story of a true friendship. In the 1914–18 war there were two men who were close friends. One was left wounded in no-man's-land between the trenches. His friend waited until darkness came, and then at the peril of his life crawled out to help him. The first words which the wounded man said were: "I knew that you would come."

In the ups and downs of life, true friendship remains the same.

The Greeks had a phrase which speaks of "time which wipes all things out", as if the mind of man were a slate, and time a sponge which passes across the slate and wipes it clean. There are friendships which vanish with the years. There are people from whom we were once inseparable, with whom nowadays we would find it difficult even to make conversation.

Of course there are friendships from which we quite inevitably grow away. But real friendships are victorious over the years. You may not see a real friend for months and even years at a time, but you can take up the friendship just where you left off.

True friendship will cross time and distance as you grow older, you will find. In fact now in your schools and your clubs, you are forming, I hope, just those sorts of friendships.

If so, they will stick!

Read Ruth 1: 1–18.

ANDY CAPP   Day Fifteen

I was speaking one day about a "handicap". One little boy thought I was talking about Andy Capp!

I once knew a child who had got one phrase of the Lord's Prayer a bit wrong. She thought it was "Harold be Thy name"!

Another little boy—perhaps a budding ornithologist—said his prayer as "Deliver us from eagles"!

And another (a train spotter?) prayed: "Lead us not into Thames Station"!

Then there was the little girl who got the line of the hymn wrong. It reads: "Weak and sinful though we be". She sang: "We can sing full though we be"!

Words can be misunderstood for all sorts of reasons. My six-year-old friend really knew Andy Capp, but perhaps wasn't so familiar with the religious words I was using. So we who teach and preach to you must think about the words we use, and learn from you the ways in which you like to be taught.

There would be nothing wrong in teaching about Jesus using a strip cartoon to do it—if it helps you.

It is the message that is important.

The medium is whatever truly helps.

Read Hosea 14: 1–2.

WHAT IS YOUR NAME?   Day Sixteen

What is your name?

I don't know of course, but I hope it is one that is important to *you*.

Chrysostom, in the fifth century, tells of one odd way of choosing a name in his day. The parents would get a number of candles. They would give each candle a name. They would then light all the candles, and the child was given the name which had been attached to the candle that burned longest!

Sometimes it has been the custom to give a child a name in a way that expressed one's faith.

Elijah means "Jahweh is my God," and this name was given to the young Elijah when Baal worship (that is idol worship) was very prevalent. In giving it to their child the parents asserted their faith. The Puritans did this in a way that reduced the whole thing to the ridiculous. The famous critic Lord Macaulay tells of the man called Tribulation Wholesome and another called Zeal-of-the-Lord Busy.

The most awful example of this is the name that the Fleet Street leather-worker, himself called Praise-God Barebones, gave to his son. He called him "If-Christ-had-not-died-for-thee-thou-wouldst-have-been-damned Barebones"!

It is good to know the meaning of your name—Margaret, the pearl; Katherine, the pure one; Jane, the grace of God; Peter, the rock; Andrew, the courageous one; Alexander, the defender; Irene, peace.

It is good to have a name to live up to.

Read 1 Kings 18: 36–40.

GOOD NAMES   Day Seventeen

It may be good, too, to have names in the family that remind us of lovely things. To have Irene—peace—in the house should be good!

David had two sons called Elishama and Eliada.
Elishama means: God hears.
Eliada means: God knows.

To have such reminders about God in his house must have been good for David.

He need never forget that God knows and God hears.

Read Genesis 32: 24–30.

CHRISTIAN NAMES   Day Eighteen

Chrysostom, who did not like the candle method one little bit, was all for giving a child one of the great saints' names and then telling the child the story of the name, so that he would become like the saint after whom he was called.

I once knew a girl called Elizabeth Margaret, who was

142

thrilled when she discovered that she bore the names of the most famous queens of Scotland and England!

I have often thought that it would be a good idea to delay naming a child finally until you could see how he or she turned out! There is not much point in giving a name like Lynette to a chunky little tomboy! It is unfortunate to saddle a small, self-effacing, diffident boy with the name Hector, greatest of the Trojans, or to call a young tough Lancelot or Gareth! There would be something to be said for waiting for a name to fit!

Nowadays one of the commonest ways is just to give the child a name you happen to like. My two grand-daughters are called Jill and Karen, for no particular reason other than that their parents liked the names.

The idea of a *Christian* name is wonderful. It is the name we have because we are Christ's boys, Christ's girls: the name we are given when we are Christ-ened, or baptised.

It is a great responsibility to have a Christian name.
We must carry it well.

Read St. Matthew 1: 18–23.

GIVE—EXTRAVAGANTLY! Day Nineteen

You like getting presents?
Of course you do!
But I once came across a man who, on his birthday, made a point of *giving* presents.
It was a good idea!

John told us the loveliest story in the Gospels about the woman who anointed Jesus' feet with the perfume (John 12: 1–8). The perfume could have been sold for three hundred silver pieces—about fifteen pounds in modern money—a colossal sum. A denarius, one of these silver pieces—about four pence—was a working man's wage for a day. That phial of perfume cost almost a year's wages!

There were extremely sensible people present who were horrified at the extravagance and who thought that the perfume should have been sold and the proceeds given to the poor.

No one loved the poor more than Jesus did—but he didn't think that. It was the sheer extravagance of the gift, the fact that it was fantastically generous and reckless, that went straight to his heart. And he promised that all the world would know about the lovely thing that this woman had done.

The value of a present lies in the fact it is an *extra*. It should cost us something to give. Presents we give just because we have to (and quite a lot of Christmas giving is really for that reason) don't really have any purpose. They should be an expression of love, and so the more extravagant the better! Which is, I feel, the point of the story of the woman with her perfume.

I know we must not be extravagant unnecessarily and certainly not spend what we haven't got. But I want to stress the sacrificial aspect of giving to someone. For it is the cost to us that really counts.

So in giving to God, David rightly said: "I will not offer to the Lord offerings which have cost me nothing."

Read St. John 12: 1–8.

ALONE AND TOGETHER   Day Twenty

Jesus liked to be alone and needed to be alone. That was why he spent his days in the wilderness, or sometimes tried to slip away from people.

But he liked company too.

He chose the Twelve that they might be with him (Mark 3: 14), and even in Gethsemane he wanted the chosen three to share his vigil; not that they could do anything, but just that they might be there (Mark 14: 32–41).

The essence of friendship is knowing when to be with someone and when to leave them, when to speak or just be there. The right time is important.

There is a famous passage in Ecclesiastes 3 about different times. He says there is a time to weep, and a time to laugh, a time to keep and a time to cast away. The "preacher" did not include in the list a time to act and a time not to act; the nearest he got to it was a time to keep silence and a time to speak, and the real essence of friendship is to know which is which.

Mary of Bethany had this sensitive awareness. She knew that there was a time when the only thing to do was to sit in silence at Jesus' feet and just be with him with no action at all (Luke 10: 42). But she also knew that there was a time to take the ointment and to anoint his feet, and so act publicly that all might see the devotion of her love (John 12: 1–8).

There are times when true friendship demands action, when just to be there and do nothing would not be an act of friendship at all. There are times when true friendship demands simply the support of the silent presence of some one.

It is in this kind of understanding that true friends are known. They sense when we should be alone. They know when we need them.

To develop that sensitivity is a very valuable thing.
I hope you will.

Read St. Matthew 10: 1–8.

MISTRANSLATIONS ...   Day Twenty-one

The Bible really is a wonderful book! Even when you mistranslate it, it says something to you!

I received a letter from someone who has lived a hard life and has still a great faith. It finished with thanksgiving and a quotation from the Authorised Version of Psalm 139: 13: "Thou hast possessed my reins."

Now I think that the writer of that letter took "reins" in the sense of the reins which guide a horse, and he took it to mean that God had guided him all through life. He was very thankful for the loving guidance of God which he found mentioned this text.

But in fact that is not the meaning of this text at all! True, any ordinary twentieth-century person would almost certainly take the word "reins" in that sense, for it is the only sense of the word that he knows. But the word here literally means the kidneys; and the meaning of the text is that God knows a man because God has formed even his inmost and his most secret parts. The Revised Standard Version has: "Thou didst form my inward parts." Moffatt has: "Thou didst form my being." Goodspeed has: "Thou didst create my vitals."

In fact this gentleman has been encouraged and strengthened by a mistranslation and a misunderstanding. But the encouragement and the strength were real.

This is not an argument for having mistranslations! No, we need all the skill and learning we can find to help us understand the Bible more. For when inspiration and scholarship get together in the Bible, it truly speaks.

But don't worry too much if a mistranslation helps you! So long as the thought is good and it spurs you to action, or makes your character better, it hasn't done too badly!

Read Psalm 139: 14–18.

... AND MISTRANSLATIONS! Day Twenty-two

Now here is an interesting thing about mistranslations. A completely mistaken doctrine of the Church was built on a mistranslation! In fact one great authority has called it "the most disastrous in idea and influence".

It is a mistranslation in John 10: 16. The Authorised Version runs: "Other sheep I have, which are not of this fold: them also I must bring, and they shall hear my voice; and there shall be one fold, and one shepherd."

In the English of the Authorised Version, the word "fold" occurs twice, but the words are quite different words in the Greek. In the first case the Greek word is *aule*, which is correctly translated "fold"; in the second case the Greek word is *poimne*, which means "flock", not "fold".

Any modern translation—Moffatt, Revised Standard Version, New English Bible—will show that the last part of the verse should read: "There will be one flock, one shepherd."

The seriousness of this mistranslation is that this is the text which Roman Catholics use to prove that there is only one Church, and that outside that Church there is no salvation. But Jesus said nothing like that. He said that there was one flock, which is a very different thing, for a flock could be distributed throughout many folds and still remain the same flock and the flock of the one owner.

There is nothing in this text which proves that there can be only one Church; there is everything in it to prove that there may be many churches but there is only one *flock* of Christ which is distributed throughout all the churches.

How did this mistranslation arise? It arose because the New Testament was first translated not directly from the Greek but from the Latin Vulgate. For some quite unknown reason Jerome, when he made the Vulgate, translated both *aule* and *poimne* by the same Latin word (*ovile*) which does not mean a fold.

So you can see how in this case a mistranslation does do harm.

You can get benefit from a mistranslation. But you can also go badly wrong!

Take care!

Read St. John 10: 1–16.

Let us think today about the Lord's Day (Sunday).

Here are, first, some facts:

The Sabbath and the Lord's Day are different days.

The Sabbath is Saturday and the Lord's Day is Sunday; the Sabbath is the last day of the week and the Lord's Day is the first day of the week. It is therefore clear that the Christian does not observe the Sabbath, and that terms such as "Sabbath School" are wrong and misleading.

The Sabbath and the Lord's Day commemorate different events.

The Sabbath remembers the rest of God after the six days of creation; the Lord's Day remembers the rising of Jesus from the dead.

The two days therefore have different objects.

The object of the Sabbath is to continue that rest which ended the work of creation. It will therefore be very properly a day when human work also stops.

The object of the Lord's Day is to make the experience of the Resurrection real today.

The first reference to the Lord's Day is in Revelation 1: 10.

By the early second century, at least in Asia Minor, the observance of the Lord's Day was universal in the Christian Church, and Ignatius could speak of Christians as no longer "sabbatising" but keeping the Lord's Day.

Now for some positive statements!

As the Lord's Day is Resurrection day, it is natural to worship on it.

The Lord's Day should be a family day, for it may be the only day of the week that the whole family can be together. Sunday dinner is not really a joke. It is much nearer to being a sacrament.

The Lord's Day should be a day of rest.

"A Sunday well-spent brings a week of content."

So value the Lord's Day!

Read St. Mark 2: 23–28.

SALVATION   Day Twenty-four

Dr. Billy Graham, the great American evangelist, tells how in an American university he and his team had been answering questions for two hours. At the end of the session one of the students said to him, "All right, tell me what you want me to do. What do I do to find God?"

In answer Billy Graham laid down what you might call four steps on the way to salvation.

"*First*," he said, "you must be willing to admit that God is, that he exists.

"*Second*, you must accept the fact that he loves you in spite of your sins, failures, and rebellion. This is why he gave his Son to die on the Cross for you.

"*Third*, you must be willing to repent of your sin. Repentance means that you confess your transgression of moral law and that you are willing to give up your sin.

"*Fourth*, you must receive Jesus Christ as your own Lord and Saviour."

This is an excellent way to think of the meaning of salvation.

God is and *God cares.*

"No astonomer can be an atheist," said one great scientist. There is a perfect order in the world. The sun observes its time; the tides do not vary; the planets never leave their courses; the same combination of the elements will always produce the same result.

The old analogy is that if you find a watch, you are bound

to deduce the existence of a watchmaker; wherever there is order, there is bound to be mind. If you find a world which has a perfect order and harmony, then you are bound to assume a world-maker. In that sense, reason insists that *God exists.*

But that does not take you very far. Such an argument does not really prove that God exists; it proves that he existed. The watchmaker who made the watch may be dead long ago. Neither does it prove that God still cares for the world, or that he has anything more to do with it.

The Christian assertion is not only that God is, but also that God cares.

That last part is very important.

That is why Jesus is so important for we see and meet God in him. We can learn from nature, but the supreme revelation of what God is like is in Jesus.

Read St. Matthew 6: 25–34.

IN TRAINING   Day Twenty-five

General Booth, the founder of the Salvation Army, and his wife, put together a training manual—as long ago as 1884.

There are several aims in it. And they help us a lot, even though it was written such a long time ago.

The training of a Salvation officer begins with *the heart*. If the heart is not right, the service won't be right. The first essential is a heart that has felt the love of God in Jesus and responded to it.

Next *the head* must be trained.

Knowledge is not everything, but the more we know, the better we are equipped to help people. You expect your teachers to know more than you do! So he must be mentally equipped for his work.

He must be able *to touch people's consciences*.

You remember what St. Paul said, "What we shouldn't do, we do and what we should do, we don't do." We must be aware of wrong in us. The officer must be able to make us feel sorry for the wrong we do.

He must be able *to give hope to the hope-less*.

Jesus was a friend of publicans, sinners, outcasts. To help those down and out is a first necessity. This may just mean giving food or a roof for the night.

Whatever it is, it is the beginning of a new life.

Read Romans 7: 15–25.

GOOD LISTENERS
Day Twenty-six

Do you find it hard to be silent?
I think most of us do!
Good listeners are scarce.

This is important in prayer. Here, too, we often talk too much.

Do we *say* too much? In any converstaion, if you talk all the time, you never hear what is being said to you—or what someone is trying to say to you! It is the same in prayer. If we do all the talking, we will never be able to listen and hear God's will for us.

"Keep silence before him" as the Bible says—sometimes.

Do we *do* too much?

In the Old Testament story the man who was enjoined to look after a prisoner captured in the battle, did this and that and the prisoner escaped. When he was called to explain he could only make the lame excuse: "As your servant was busy here and there he was gone" (1 Kgs. 20: 40).

We can be so busy doing things that we miss the important things in life.

Martha, in the incident at Bethany we have already referred to, was, as the Bible says, "careful and troubled about many things"—getting the meal ready, running the house. Mary sat at Jesus' feet and listened.

Both did good things, though Martha felt a bit irritated by Mary's inactivity! But Jesus felt what she did was important.

Sometimes to be quiet, to think and to listen, is right and good.

We often do very little of real good when we think we are very busy!

Read St. Luke 10; 38-42.

MANY GIFTS   Day Twenty-seven

How I depend on other people!

If my car goes wrong, I shout for help.

I could not do my work for a day without my hearing aid. When it goes wrong, there is someone there to mend it in a matter of hours.

It takes so many people in the background to enable any of us to go on doing our work. And the trouble is that we so often take them completely for granted.

You have only to think of so simple a thing as how we get to work in the morning. How different it would be if there was no wife or mother to get us out of bed in time, to get a breakfast cooked and on to the table, and to see us out of the door in time to catch our bus or train. In fact, we seldom remember that the bus or train has a driver!

How we depend on these people in the background. We tend to consider certain people very important in life—footballers, pop stars, politicians, and so on. But we ought to be grateful for the mass of ordinary people doing ordinary jobs without whom we would be in great difficulty.

"There are many gifts, but one spirit is behind them all," says St. Paul.

Some may have what seem important gifts ... the ability to sing, to teach, to look after business, etc. Often ordinary gifts are under-valued. How important, for example, is the gift of friendship, a sense of humour, the ability to make a cup of tea?

The Christian mission began over an evening meal in an upper room long ago. We don't know who looked after the hospitality that night.

But their contribution was invaluable.

They helped us to inherit Christianity.

Read 1 Corinthians 12: 4–13.

SHOW ME YOUR HANDS   Day Twenty-eight

Tolstoy has a story of a nobleman who always kept open house. At evening anyone could come and have a meal at his hospitable table. And when anyone came, he was never turned away, but there was one test. The nobleman always said, "Show me your hands," and, if the hands were rough and scarred with toil, then the man was given a seat of honour at the top of the table, but if the hands were soft and flabby, then his place was low at the foot of the table.

Dr. Jacks tells the story of an Irish navvy. He was a simple man, and one day someone asked him what he would say if, when he died, he was stopped at the heavenly gates and asked if he could produce any reason why he should be allowed in. He paused for a moment, and then looked down at his spade with its blade polished and sharpened with constant work until it looked almost like stainless steel. "I think," he said, "I'll just show them my spade."

Jacks added that when he wrote his many books he always wore an old jacket, the right sleeve of which had become all tattered and worn from the constant friction with his desk as he wrote. "I wonder," he said, "if my old frayed coat sleeve will get me in?"

There is a lot of value in honest toil. Sir Winston Churchill, in his famous plea in the Second World War asked for "blood, sweat, tears and toil". To give real hard work is to create real value in life.

The boy who becomes the man who is willing to do an honest day's work will indeed be the conqueror. There are some victories we cannot win, but the victory of honest work is open to us all,

Read Paslm 24.

HOE HANDLES
Day Twenty-nine

Let's say a little more about honest work because it is important, not least today when the wage for the job seems more important so often than honest work.

Apolo Kivebulaya was one of the great saints of the African Church and in the book *African Saint*, Anne Luck told his story.

One of the most characteristic stories tells how he arrived at Mboga in the Congo. He was not the first Christian missionary to arrive there. Two African missionaries had been there before him, but they had had to leave, because the people would not give them any food. These two former missionaries had been members of the proud Baganda tribe in which menial work is for women and slaves. So, when the people of Mboga refused them food, they had been far too proud to cultivate the land themselves and so they had to starve or go.

Apolo knew this, and he was well prepared to grow his own food. As he passed through the patches of forest on his way to Mboga, he stopped to cut some hoe handles to be ready to get to work on some patch of ground whenever he arrived. When Tabaro, the ruler of Mboga, saw Apolo coming into the village carrying his hoe handles at the ready he said, "Here is a man who is going to conquer."

A hoe handle may be an odd sign for a conqueror, and an odd crest for a victor, but the very sight of it marked out Apolo as the man who would conquer. And why? For the simple yet sufficient reason that here was a man who was clearly prepared to do an honest day's work.

What the world needs more than anything else is men who are ready, prepared and willing to do an honest day's work.

Read St. Luke 10: 1–7.

HONEST WORK   Day Thirty

In the story of Apolo, about which we thought yesterday, hoe handles made it clear to the Congo people that Apolo was prepared to work as well as preach.

Under the Jewish law the rabbis were the greatest scholars and teachers of their day; they were the equivalent of the modern professor. But every Jewish rabbi had to have a trade. No rabbi could take any money for teaching and preaching at all. He had to earn his living by working at some trade. So we find rabbis who were tailors, carpenters, perfumers, barbers; and we know the trade of one who might have become one of the greatest of all Jewish rabbis, if he had not become one of the greatest of Christians, for we know that Paul was a tent-maker, or, as the word probably came to mean, a leatherworker.

The rabbi had to work with his hands as well as with his brain and with his words.

Honest work is valuable to men.
It is we believe valued too by God.

Read 2 Thessalonians 3: 6–10.

155

> I read
> In a book
> That a man called
> Christ
> Went about doing good.
> It is very disconcerting
> To me
> That I am so easily satisfied
> With just
> Going about.

In the Bible there are two kinds of "goings about" spoken of. Satan came to the assembly of the sons of God from going to and fro upon the earth (Job 1: 7), and in Peter's letter the Devil is said to "prowl about" seeking whom he may devour (1 Pet. 5: 8). And on the other hand Jesus of Nazareth was said to have "gone about doing good" (Acts 10: 38).

These are, as it were, the two opposite poles. The Devil goes about seeking whom he may devour; Jesus Christ went about doing good.

Kagawa, who wrote the poem above, speaks about "just going about". But in point of fact it is impossible to go about, as it were, and do nothing! Your very presence brings something with it; you have an effect on everyone you meet, even on everyone you pass on the street.

We can, for example, go about encouraging.

No one could desire a finer epitaph than: "He was a great encourager."

"Courage! Keep your heart up!" was a word that was often on Jesus' lips, for the word which the Authorised Version translated, "Be of good cheer!" means just exactly that.

"Courage!" Jesus said to the man who was sick with the palsy (Matt. 9: 2).

"Courage!" he said to the scared woman who crept up and touched him in the crowd (Matt. 9: 22).

"Courage!" he said to the disciples terrified in the storm on the lake (Matt. 14: 27).

"Courage!" said the Risen Christ to St. Paul when he was up against it in Jerusalem and when there seemed every reason to despair (Acts 23: 11).

Anyone who encourages his fellow-men is walking in his Master's footsteps, and speaking with his Master's accent.

Read St. Matthew 14: 22–27.

MONTH SIX

Rusty is our bull terrier. He likes to be at my feet when I am working.

No one ever comes here without a tumultuous reception from Rusty. And, of course, at mealtimes he is usually hanging around near the table, hopefully!

But Rusty is not here just now. He has had an experience which has rather upset him!

We are due to be away for a few days and Rusty is not allowed to come. So Rusty had to have his board and lodging fixed up in kennels where they will be very kind and good to him.

One day last week Rusty was taken to the kennels, but refused to enter them. He shook and shivered and wept and slipped his collar and ran away. In the end he had to be bodily lifted and carried in and left.

Rusty was of course broken-hearted and terrified at leaving the people he knows and loves. But it is all right. We phoned to see how he was getting on (you would think he was an invalid in a nursing home!) and he has settled down and is quite happy.

I have just been reading an article in a newspaper which horrified me. This article says that every day stray and homeless cats and dogs are picked up. But in the summer months, June, July and August, every week they are picked up literally by the hundred and many roam the streets homeless until they starve to death.

This is because there are people who, when they go on holiday, simply turn their animals out and make no provision for them.

This article goes on to say that quite often children get a present of a kitten or a puppy for Christmas or for a birthday. For a week or two, or a month or two, some of them are thrilled with their new friend. Then they get tired of it, and the animal is put out. It is left to wander and get lost, and to get run over, perhaps, or starve.

I hope none of you will ever be cruel to an animal. The fact that it just can't complain makes the cruelty worse.

Christians can't be cruel to animals.
Christians can't be cruel.

Read Isaiah 11: 1–9.

GOD AND THE ANIMALS   Day Two

Let's think a bit more about animals, for I just cannot stand cruelty to them.

Here is a lovely prayer for animals. It comes from Dr. Leslie Weatherhead's book, *Why Do Men Suffer?*

Hear our humble prayer, O God, for our friends the animals. In thy hand is the soul of every living thing, and we bless thee that thou carest for the dumb creatures of the earth. We bless and praise thee for thy joy in their beauty and grace, and we desire to share thy love for all of them. Accept our prayer specially for animals who are suffering; for all that are over-worked and underfed and cruelly treated; for all wistful creatures in captivity that beat against their bars; for any that are hunted or lost or deserted or frightened or hungry; for all that are in pain or dying; for all that must be put to death. We entreat for them all thy mercy and pity and for those who deal with them we ask a heart of compassion, and gentle hands, and kindly words. Make us ourselves to be true friends to animals and so to share the blessing of the merciful. For the sake of thy Son the tenderhearted Jesus Christ our Lord. Amen.

God will not think it strange that we pray for the animals. The prophet Hosea heard God speak to him about the last days when the golden age would come: "And I will make for you a covenant on that day with the beasts of the field and the birds of the air, and the creeping things of the ground" (Hos. 2: 18, R.S.V.)

In the vision of the perfect time there would be perfect friendship between man and the beasts.

Cruelty is always an ugly thing; and cruelty to animals in their dumb helplessness is an especially ugly thing.

The love of God is the love that stretches out over man and beast.

Read Proverbs 30: 24–31.

ADVERTISEMENTS   Day Three

Have your heard of the *Strand Magazine*?

It was very famous because in it the Sherlock Holmes stories first appeared.

But in the copy I happened to pick up, what interested me were the advertisement pages. There were many of them, but none contained any advertisement for coffee or cigarettes and very few for alcohol.

I found the advertisements it did have, very interesting. They fell into various classes.

There were many advertisements for *food* and for *clothes*. Well, these are our basic needs. Men need to know what they are going to eat and what they are going to put on.

There were many advertisements for *medicines*, for *toothpaste*, for *medicines for babies*, for *reducing treatments* and *slimming diets*, and for *electrical machines* which were guaranteed to cure all ills! People, then as now, were interested in their health.

Here are some lessons to be drawn from this experience:

The basic, fundamental needs of people do not change. 'Boys will be boys'—and girls girls—in every age. The things around us change, but we don't, when we really look at ourselves.

That is why Jesus is (as we said earlier) "the same yesterday, today and for ever". He meets basic spiritual needs in every age.

There were then fewer advertisements for *luxuries*. I'm afraid our sophisticated age asks for more and more luxuries—without finding happiness through them.

"Man does not live by bread alone". Over and over again, we find this out.

In those days the advertisements offered us something. They were designed to meet a need. Nowadays they set out to *create the need*. And so discontent is created.

How right the Bible is: "There is great gain in godliness with content" (1 Tim. 6: 6).

Possessions, in the end, are comparatively unimportant.

Read St. Luke 12: 13–21.

THE SCHOOL OF LIFE   Day Four

When Sir Walter Scott was a lad, an accident kept him from his usual activities so he had time to look at the books of old Scots stories and histories. Afterwards, an old friend who had watched what had happened said, "He was makin' himsel' a' the time; but he didna ken maybe what he was about till the years had passed."

You may not fully understand his Scottish "lingo", but he is really saying this. All he was doing and all that happened to him was part of the process of God making him into something of value to people.

What are you going to do with your life? Is God preparing you for it?

Perhaps there are things you have to learn or experiences you have to undergo that in the end will seem to have played a part in making your character.

St. Paul says of the law that it was a schoolmaster to lead him to Christ. Life's experiences, in God's providence, can fulfil that purpose.

We all live in the school of life. Everything we learn in it can become part of the teaching we need to live.

See God in it all.
He is making you all the time.

Read 2 Timothy 2: 1–7.

WET BLANKET OR RED FLAG   Day Five

Are you a red-flag-waver or a wet-blanket-provider?

There is no doubt which I would prefer you to be ... if you understand what the red flag/wet blanket choice means!

W. L. Watkinson tells how he was walking along the promenade in Brighton with his little grandson. They met an older minister who was sadly disgruntled. Nothing in this world was right; everything and everybody was all wrong, and to make matters worse he was suffering from a slight touch of sunstroke.

The little grandson had been silently listening. When they had left the gloom-stricken old man and walked on for a short distance, the little grandson looked up at W. L. Watkinson and said, "Grand-dad, I hope that you never suffer from a sunset."

The red flag, in our context, stands for joy and encouragement. The wet blanket stands for discouragement.

We say of someone who seems to want to extinguish all our enthusiasm, "Oh, he is a wet blanket". And we don't really appreciate him (or her!) very much.

The red flag is a joyful symbol. It implies enthusiasm and encouragement. Perhaps the little boy was right — even if the words he used sound a bit strange. If you are a Christian, you should be someone who stands for the sunrise, the beginning of new things, not the sunset which, though lovely, can feel a bit sad.

So help, lend a hand, befriend, encourage. These are the things that are symbolised by the red flag.

Don't be a wet blanket!
Wave that flag!

Read Isaiah 52: 7–10.

USE YOUR MEMORY!   Day Six

Have you a good memory?

If you have (and you should have at your your age!) you are very lucky.

The important thing is to use memory to the best advantage. There are things worth remembering and there are things that are not.

I feel (though you may disagree) that the time spent memorising the books of the Bible would be better spent memorising some great passages from it—passages like Psalm 23 ("The Lord is my shepherd, I shall not want"), Psalm 46 ("God is our refuge and strength"), 1 Corinthians 13 ("The greatest of these is love"), the last part of Romans 8 ("Nothing shall separate us . . ."), St. John 14 "(In my Father's house are many mansions . . .") and some of the parables.

In a crisis in life, it will be comparatively little comfort to know whether the book of Isaiah follows or precedes the book of Jeremiah! But to be able to go over in one's memory, a passage from the Bible could help a lot.

Use your memory well!
It is a great asset!

Read Romans 8: 35–39.

YOUR COMPUTER   Day Seven

It is a rather frightening thought that your memory registers everything you do in life.

I don't mean that you can recall everything, but it is all there! It is really the most marvellous computer of all.

H. G. Wells said that there are three main faults which affect the mind and the memory. There is, first, inexact reception; second, bad storage; third, uncertain accessibility.

"Inexact reception" means we need to concentrate more.

"Bad storage" is the storing up of the wrong things.

"Uncertain accessibility" is the difficulty we sometimes have in locating a particular piece of information in our memory.

"I can't remember names" is a common complaint in people of *my* age!

There are, too, things that we don't want to remember! To forget a "date" may mean you didn't really want to go rather than that you couldn't remember!

The way to benefit from memory is to store it with things worth remembering—or as the Bible would say "the things that are good and lovely and of good report!" to use a phrase I have mentioned before.

If you remember these things, you can think on these things and have great and lasting benefit from them.

Read Psalm 77: 1–11.

KINDNESS Day Eight

What people need above all else is a helping hand to lift them up.

So said the Roman writer, Seneca, long ago.

Kindness is important in life.

Charles Kingsley wrote in "A Farewell to C. E. G.":

Be good, sweet maid, and let who will be clever;
Do noble things, not dream them all day long;
And so make Life, and Death, and that For Ever;
One grand sweet song.

And I think that it was the same poet who gave the advice:

> Do the work that's nearest,
> Though it's dull at whiles,
> Helping, when we meet them,
> Lame dogs over stiles.

One of the greatest scholars under whom it was my privilege ever to sit was John E. McFadyen, who taught so many of my generation Hebrew, and opened our eyes to the wonder of the Old Testament. But it is not "Johnnie's" scholarship that we who knew him remember; it was his kindness.

I remember a college football match at which Johnnie was present—he always came to them. One of our Glasgow boys was hurt—he was assistant in a certain church with responsibility for services in a mission. That evening there was a knock at his door. He opened it to find Johnnie on the doorstep. "You were knocked out at the match today," said Johnnie (it was Saturday), "and I've come to see if I could take your services for you tomorrow."

It is kindness that matters.

It is kindness not cleverness that the world needs.

'Inasmuch as you have done it unto one of the least of these my brethren you have done it unto me" (Matt. 25: 40).

Read St. Matthew 25: 31–45.

CHANGE OF ATTITUDE   Day Nine

In his book, *A New Mind for a New Age*, Dr. Alan Walker tells of a plaque in a coal-mining village near Manchester, commemorating a mining disaster. It reads as follows: "In the year 1832 the Lord terribly visited the colliery of Robert Clark and the above named were called to meet their Maker," and there is a list of twenty-three persons who died in the disaster.

Few people would put the blame on God for a mining disaster nowadays, I'm glad to say. But what is more staggering is that every one of the twenty-three "people" who died were younger than you. They were all under nine years old.

We have Christianity to thank for this change of attitude. We just can't let this kind of thing happen to children now, that other ages allowed. We value children today—because our faith teaches us to do this.

Aristotle the great Greek writer said: "Master and slave have nothing in common; a slave is a living tool, just as a tool is an inanimate slave."

Varro is equally definite. Writing a treatise for the Romans on agriculture, he divides the instruments of agriculture into three classes—the articulate, the inarticulate, and the mute: "the articulate comprising the slaves, the inarticulate comprising the cattle and the mute comprising the vehicles". The only difference between a slave and a beast or a cart was that a slave could talk!

When Lord Shaftesbury was asked why he toiled so hard for chimney-sweeps and factory workers and coal miners, he answered: "I have undertaken this task, because I regard the objects of it as being, like ourselves, created by the same God, redeemed by the same Saviour, and destined for the same immortality."

He showed that Christianity just won't allow the old attitudes. It is inhuman and so it is un-Christian.

There are many of us who have to be very grateful for all Christianity has done.

Read James 1: 22–27.

Looking into a mirror can create many different reactions.

Do you remember the story of Narcissus, the handsome young Greek, who was not much concerned for anyone else, but he did like himself.

Looking into a pool of clear water one day, he saw his own reflection and he fell in love with himself. He just wanted to keep looking and looking at his own lovely appearance. But he was so entranced with himself that, wholly occupied in gazing at his own reflection, he pined away and died. At death, he was changed into the Narcissus flower. And the truth in that story must never be missed.

Self-admiration is the death of the soul. To admire ourselves as we are is to have no wish to change. And with those who don't want to change, the soul is dead.

Be careful about too much self-admiration!

A famous cartoonist drew a little man on a vast pile of books, looking into a mirror. The books were labelled history, philosophy, biology, theology, etc.

The little man was clearly an academic who knew the contents of all the books and probably understood them. As he looked in the mirror, there was sheer bewilderment, and above his head there was a question mark. He understood everything—except himself!

We are often a puzzle to ourselves. Perhaps that is why the principle "Know thyself" is all important.

To look in the mirror can be a useful thing to do if it helps us to see our faults and failings and makes us want to have a better or even a new image.

Jesus can, of course, help us to that new image.
He makes all things—and people—new.

Read 2 Corinthians 5: 12–17.

Man has power today such as no other generation ever possessed.

Distance has been annihilated, and space is on the way to being spanned.

The means of "mass communication" make it almost as easy to speak to a continent as to a single individual.

Speeds which would once have been thought incredible are commonplace.

Measured in terms of sheer destruction, the power which man controls is like a devilish and satanic miracle.

It is this power which has presented man with a life and death problem.

Bertrand Russell said, "Science as technique has conferred a sense of power; man is much less at the mercy of his environment than he was in former times."

This *power* has given us all great problems. The problem is not now the acquisition of power. The problem is the use of power. All power is in itself quite neutral. It is neither good nor bad. It has potential for goodness and for evil, for blessing and for destruction.

There is no use in abolishing distance and bringing the ends of the earth together, if they are to be brought together in bitterness and strife.

If speed of travel simply means that peoples and nations can get more quickly at each other's throats, there is little use in it.

If the greatest powers men can command are to be concentrated on destruction, it were better not to have discovered them.

"It is not by might or by power, but by my Spirit, saith the Lord of Hosts." So wrote Micah.

Power in itself is neither good nor evil.

It is what we do with it that matters.

That is why it is so important what kind of people we will grow up to be.

That is why to be "Christian" is important.

Read Zechariah 4: 1–6.

SITTERS DOWN Day Twelve

Two things I have read recently make me worried. I would like you to think about them.

The first is a reference in an article in *The Lancet* (a magazine for doctors) by Dr. Reginald Passmore, Reader in Physiology in Edinburgh University.

Dr. Passmore says that a new species of man is emerging in the West—a species which takes in too much food (often of the wrong sort) in relation to his energy output, and becomes diseased as a result. He calls this species *Homo sedentarius*, which literally means "sitting-down man".

Here is the description of the kind of life that many people, perhaps most of us, lead. We are driven to (work) school sitting down in a bus, train or motor car. We sit at a desk. We eat meals which are too large and too rich. We are driven home again at night. And perhaps we spend a lot of the evening half-sitting, half-lying in a chair watching television.

It isn't good for us!

Read Proverbs 6: 6–11.

WITNESSES Day Thirteen

The second thing that worries me I came across in an article by the well-known journalist, Arthur Helliwell.

Mr. Helliwell had been touring America and had been seeing life there. He tells us that in relation to income tax returns and other returns, a new profession is appearing, the profession of witness.

All over the United States, [he goes on to say], men are now employed as "witnesses", and a witness is a man who does no work. He simply watches work being done by giant robots; by Frankenstein monsters with iron hands and steel fingers that can work faster, more precisely and more efficiently than any man, by delicate machines that can assemble wrist-watches or wrap and pack fragile chocolates; and by electronic "brains" with eerie memories that can perform half a million intricate calculations in sixty seconds.

All the robot needs is to be started, stopped—and watched, by "witnesses", men who for most of their working day never have to take their hands out of their pockets.

There are robots so sensitive that they do not even need to be switched off and on, but will respond to the sound of the human voice. So in Chicago there is a robot which can turn out one thousand transistor sets a day, and it needs only two men to tend it. In New York there is a bottling plant which can wash, refill, cap and crate two hundred thousand bottles a day with a total staff of three men to watch it.

The "witness" is a "workman" who can do his day's work by sitting watching, and never doing a thing.

These "witnesses" feel very dangerous to me. It makes me think again, how vital it is that we should be *Christians* today—Christ's men, Christ's women, Christ's boys, Christ's girls, with a Christian attitude to power and to people.

Jesus said *you* are my witnesses.

Whatever else we must be or do, we must be that today in our strange new world.

Read Acts 1: 1–8.

173

Do you like construction kits?

It can be fun building something yourself, can't it? You can feel proud when you have been able to "do-it-yourself"!

Construction kits, for me, are parables of life.

God does not give us a completed life; he gives us the raw materials out of which to make a life.

God gives us ourselves, with all our gifts and our abilities. He gives us the world, with all its beauty, its bounty, and its resources. He gives us the people we live with; and he says to us, "Out of all these things, make a life that is worthwhile."

It is never God's way to do things for us; it is always his way to enable us to do things for ourselves.

To succeed with your kit, you need however to do one thing—follow the instructions!

Life is like that too.

God gives us the raw materials of life, and gives us the instructions how to turn them into a real and worthwhile life. He gives us his law and his commandments in his book; a conscience within to tell us what to do and what not to do; the guidance of his Holy Spirit; and he gives us Jesus, to be both our example and our power.

God has given us the materials, the rules and instructions to follow; and God has given us his Son to help us to do things we could never do ourselves, and to make the life we could never construct ourselves.

Build well!

Read Exodus 20: 1–17.

A HOUSE OF YOUR OWN   **Day Fifteen**

Francis of Assisi loved mountains.

St. Paul says he went to Arabia to be alone.

Jesus spent forty days and forty nights in the wilderness—alone.

When you are young, you don't feel this is so important but as you grow older, I am sure you will.

The need to have "a place of your own" or "a house of your own" can be very necessary!

Have you read the book for children called *A Little House of your Own*? It is by Beatrice Schenk de Regniers who says:

> This is the important thing to remember . . .
> Everyone has to have a little house of his own.
> Every boy has to have his own little house.
> Every girl should have a little house to herself.

Perhaps the house is under the dining-room table; or in the bushes in the garden; or in a big box, or even behind a funny mask. It doesn't really matter where. The important thing is that is is *your* house. And even our friends shouldn't come in unless we ask them.

Virginia Woolf said that all she asked from life was a room of her own.

James Agate, talking of the continual bustle of entertainment on a visit to America, writes, "Here the bustle takes the form of your not being alone; a continual restless button-holing all the time . . . It doesn't seem to occur to anybody that one may like occasionally to be left alone for five minutes . . ."

Think on these things. You may not value them now but you might do so later.

We need to be alone sometimes—*to think*.
We need to be alone sometimes—*to serve others better*.
We need to be alone sometimes—*to think about God*.

At least all great people of faith have felt this need very much.

Read St. Matthew 4: 1–11 (The Temptations).

A BOOK OF WITNESS

What is your favourite book in the Bible?

It might be *St. Mark* because it tells the story of Jesus' life so clearly.

Or *St. John* because it tells that same story in a very special way.

Or *the Psalms* because of their beauty.

Or one of the "history" books of the *Old Testament* because they are exciting.

Or the thrilling book of *Daniel*—what adventures he had!

I don't think any of you would choose *Philemon*.

Unless you wanted to choose one because it is short!

In many ways the letter to Philemon is the strangest book in the New Testament. What is a little personal letter about a runaway slave named Onesimus doing in the New Testament?

There is no teaching and no "theology" in it. It is a little personal letter about a slave who had stolen from his master, and run away and who, with St. Paul, had somehow made good again, so that at last he was living up to his name Onesimus, which means "the useful one".

How did that letter get into the new Testament?

We cannot tell for sure, but we can guess. Scholars believe that it was in Ephesus about A.D. 90 that St. Paul's letters were first collected and edited and issued to the public as a book. Now some years after that Ignatius, the Bishop of Antioch, was writing letters to the Churches of Asia, as he was being taken to Rome as a prisoner—to be flung to the beasts in the arena.

Amongst the letters there is one to Ephesus which pays

rare tribute to the Bishop of Ephesus, and to his beautiful nature and the usefulness of his life—just like his name.

And what is the name of this Bishop of Ephesus? It is Onesimus.

There are scholars who believe that the runaway slave, Onesimus, and the bishop, Onesimus, are one and the same person. They believe that when St. Paul's letters to Ephesus were collected Onesimus insisted that this little letter to Philemon must go in, that all men might know what once he had been and what Jesus Christ had done for him.

So Philemon is a book of witness.
It's a short story.
But an important one.
It speaks of one man's faith.

Read St. Paul's letter to Philemon.

MOTHER   Day Seventeen

Let's think about Mother (we can't really think too often about her in my opinion!)

The Bible is rich in mothers. There is Rebekah the mother of Jacob (Gen. 27). There is Hannah the mother of Samuel (1 Sam. 1). There is the anonymous mother of Peter's wife who served Jesus with a meal (Mark 1: 29–31). There is Eunice, Timothy's mother (2 Tim. 1: 15). And there is Mary, the mother of Jesus.

Mothers have no "trade unions"!

We get a good deal of industrial trouble about "who does what". But Mum knows nothing about "demarcation" disputes. She does what has to be done willingly!

And mother's hours would cause a strike in most other occupations! We talk sometimes about the "working" man but mother's day can be from six-thirty in the morning to midnight.

An eight hour day?
Paid overtime?
Five weeks holidays?
None of it applies to mother.
She is tireless though often tired.
She is thoughtful, and we sometimes forget to be thoughtful to her.

We just couldn't do without mother!
Bless her!

Read St. Luke 2: 41–52.

KEEP MOVING Day Eighteen

You modern schoolchildren are great travellers!
I envy you!
When I was your age, it wasn't easy to go off on your own especially to far away places.
But modern young people are hardened pilgrims!

My grand-daughter Karen, when she was seven, went off to Ireland where she was to spend her holidays. She went by boat from Stranraer all by herself. True, she would be looked after on the boat and she would be met at Larne, but I'm pretty sure that at seven I wouldn't have made that journey!

My daughter Jane went off to France on her own when a teenager. True, we knew the people she was going to, and she was met at Paris, but I very much doubt if, at her age, I would have gone off with so much confidence.

I knew a young man who, when still at the university, made the most incredible journeys. On one occasion his brother drove him to the nearest motorway and left him to hitch a lift just anywhere. The boy finished up in Salonika! And the only money he spent on travel was for the boat from Dover to the Continent.

What I like about this is that you show faith.

There is the faith you have in yourself—your ability to cope.

There is the faith your parents have in you—they trust you.

There is your faith in the trustworthiness of other people. You believe people are essentially trustworthy.

In fact it is sad that hi-jacking and violence have affected that basic trust.

I think you all benefit in two ways from this adventurous spirit.

First you learn to be international in your thinking. This is good. We must think like this in our small world.

Second your travelling helps to make war less likely for as our knowledge of other nations grows, war should be less likely.

Keep travelling!
It is good for you, for us, for the world!

Read Genesis 12: 1–9

HAVE A GO! Day Nineteen

If a thing is worth doing, it is worth doing badly!

This sounds a strange thing to say! What I am doing is to try and encourage you to "have a go" at something big.

For instance there is nothing quite like the D'Oyley Carte performance of the Gilbert and Sullivan operas. A performance by that company is as near perfection as any human production can possibly be.

In contrast with that, I well remember our school performances! There would be a girl singing Frederick's part in *The Pirates of Penzance* because the school hadn't any boy tenors. The curtain would stick when it was supposed to open on the scene. And so on. But in the hearts of many of us in Dalziel High School,* it put a love for these operas that time has done nothing to lessen.

No school could possibly perform these operas like the D'Oyley Carte Company. We did them badly, yet we got one of the treasures of life out of them.

We do not stop playing golf because we cannot score like Tony Jacklin.

We do not stop playing the piano because we will never be concert pianists.

We do not stop preaching because we will never be Spurgeons.

It is worth aiming high even if it seems beyond us.

The choir *ought* to have a go at the really great music.

The preacher *ought* to attempt the great and difficult subject.

The congregation *ought* to launch out on this or that impossible scheme.

If it is worth doing, it is worth doing badly.

But—and it is a big but—it is also true that *the thing must be done, as well as we can possibly do it.*

Let us "have a go" at the big thing, so long as it is still done as well as we can possibly do it, within our limitations.

Read Nehemiah 2: 15–20.

GOAL! Day Twenty

How often we hear this word shouted rapturously on our TV set in "The Big Match" or on "Match of the Day"!

A goal is essential in life as well as football.

Without a goal, an aim, we never really get down to things or get them done.

That is why we need school exams. If we have to pass a test, we will work harder. We need this goal!

* In Motherwell, Scotland, Dr. Barclay's home town.

But the goal does something more. It sets us a test—a measuring rod for our success. Are we really progressing? Do we really improve?

We need a goal to answer these questions.

The goal we have should be, if anything, just beyond our reach. To have a goal which is too easy doesn't "stretch" us as we need to be stretched.

If you are going to fulfil your "potential", you need a real goal.

Jesus is our goal as Christians. "I press towards the mark for the prize of the high calling of God in Jesus," said Paul. He had his goal.

Press on then to your goal—always "looking unto Jesus" (Heb. 12:2).

Read Philippians: 3: 7-14

HOME

"Home, sweet home" goes the song.
"There's no place like home".
Do you agree?

If you like dogs, you will like Lord Byron's view of home.

'Tis sweet to hear the watchdog's honest bark,
Bay deep-mouthed welcome as we draw near home;
'Tis sweet to know there is an eye will mark
Our coming, and look brighter when we come.

Or you remember Robert Louis Stevenson's lines to S. R. Crockett, written away in the South Seas, far from the Scotland he loved and which for his health's sake he could never see.

Be it granted me to behold you again in dying,
Hills of home! and to hear again the call;
Hear about the graves of the martyrs the peewees
    crying,
And hear no more at all.

Do you remember the story in the Bible about Hadad the Edomite who, when he was a little child, was taken in exile to Egypt? He was well treated there, but the day came when it was safe for him to go home.

"Let me go so that I may return to my own country," he said to Pharaoh. And Pharaoh, who had loved him and treated him well said, "What is it that you find wanting in my country?" And Hadad answered, "Nothing, but do, pray, let me go" (1 Kgs. 11: 21, 22).

Yes, there really is no place like home.
Value yours!

Read 1 Kings 11: 14–22 (The story of Hadad).

DO-IT-YOURSELF   Day Twenty-Two

Are you good at "do-it-yourself" things?
Some people I know do the most wonderful things to their houses. And they enjoy doing it. For there is no greater satisfaction in life than to feel you have created something yourself.

I have a friend who decided to try woodwork. Most people, when they embark on woodwork, start with something like a pipe-rack; my friend's first production was a most elaborate, built-in, fitted wardrobe for the bedroom! There is nothing like starting in a big way!

Don't laugh at the boy or girl who tries to make something; they are finding *the joy of creation*.
It is thrilling to hold in your hand something which *you have made*. However many books you may write one day,

you will still get a thrill when you hold in your hand the finished new book. However long a craftsman may have been at his craft, his heart still beats faster when he sees his work finished.

To know the joy of creation is to share the joy of God, for it was at creation that, in Job's magnificent phrase:
    The morning stars sang together,
    And all the sons of God shouted for joy (Job 38: 7)
This joy in the product is the joy of God. Again and again in the old creation story we come on the phrase: "And God saw that it was good" (Gen. 1: 10, 18, 25, 31).

If you refuse to use your gifts, you miss the greatest thrill of life, the sheer joy of making something, the pride in the product, and the thrill of seeing others using what *your* hands and *your* mind have made.

Do it yourself!
In a big way!

Read Genesis 1: 26–31.

RAW MATERIAL   Day Twenty-three

Your "instincts" are important.
Without them you couldn't live, because they are the things that make us do the very necessary things we have to do.

There is *the instinct of self-preservation*, or survival. If you didn't have it you might not see that approaching bus, or walk carefully along a mountain ridge. So we need that one!

There is the instinct to get for ourselves: *the instinct of acquisitiveness*. If we use this rightly, we will be ambitious in the right sense. It will help us to save for the future, build a home, keep our family, and so on.

If we use it badly, it will simply become greed. The miser who never shares and never gives is the example of that instinct gone wrong.

There is *the instinct of sex*. This can produce the loveliest things in life—love between us and someone who means everything to us, the love that creates a baby. But so often the instinct is abused and spoiled. It becomes just lust. And when the instinct of sex becomes that, it is not what God meant it to be.

Instincts are what you might call the "raw material of life". What you do with them is all-important.

Let the knowledge you have of Jesus and *his* way help *you* to use this "raw material" well.

Read St. Matthew 7: 24–29.

WHAT WOULD *YOU* MISS?   Day Twenty-four

What do you think you would miss most in life?
It is a difficult question because we never really know the things until we miss them.
I think the things I miss most are what you might call the simple things.

I would miss my *home*.
I've already said quite a lot about the value of home. I just say it again. Life without home is the bleakest prospect I can conceive.

I would miss *friends*.

I like the saying of the simple Greek who was on the edge, as it were, of the circle of Socrates and the great ones. One day someone asked him for what he most wished to thank the gods. He answered, "That, being what I am, I have had the friends I have."

184

I would miss *work*.

Dr. Hugh Martin once wrote that the saddest words in all Shakespeare are: "Othello's occupation's gone."

John Wesley prayed the famous prayer: "Let me not live to be useless."

To lose work is tragedy.

That is why redundancy and unemployment can be a very terrible thing to happen to a man—or woman.

I would miss *health*.

When illness restricts us in what we can do, however little the limitation, we miss so much all that full health means.

Let us thank God for the simplest things.

Let us thank God for health.

Let us thank God for home and loved ones.

Let us thank God for friends.

Above all let us thank God for a task to do, for the strength of body, the skill of hand and the ability of mind to do it.

Read 2 Timothy 1: 6–14, especially verse 14 ("keep").

SLIMMING
Day Twenty-five

This problem of mine won't be a problem for you—even for the girls, who, I know, like to keep slim!

I have had to diet and I have learned a lot from it.

I have learned the simple but hard fact, that to lose weight, I must stop eating forbidden things. There is no short cut here—as there isn't to all the valuable things of life.

I have learned how dangerous it is to make little exceptions to the rule!

Someone hands you a plate of biscuits and says with a smile, "One won't hurt you!"

Someone offers you the chocolates and says appealingly, "Just one!"

Someone says, "Go on! Take a spoonful of sugar in your tea, just for energy!"

If you give in to this "you're sunk"!

There is no half-way house. You either take the things, or you don't take them. The little relaxations are fatal.

When you take a decision you have to take it. No half-way house, and no let-up, just as in a diet.

I have learned that the worst enemies are those who want to be kind to you.

They are the people who encourage you to take just one—"it can't do any harm".

How unwise love and kindness can be! I think it was Seneca who said: *Ama fortiter!* "Love courageously." If you love a person, the love must be strong, not sentimental. The best sympathy is a bracing, not an enervating thing.

"Yield not to temptation".

The way to say "no" is to say "NO!"

The minute we begin to waver, we are nearer to giving in.

In other words, we must have self discipline in life.

Read Numbers 22 (the story of Balaam, the man who wavered).

PRIDE   Day Twenty-six

The worst feature of my success at slimming is that I have become much too proud.

I met a man today who said rather a wise thing to me. He said to me, "I've been reading about your slimming successes!" "Yes," I said, "I've removed two and a half stones in three months." He smiled at me: "I think you ought to write a piece about pride!" he said.

He was quite right, because I was really much too pleased with myse!f!

We are apt to be pleased with ourselves over the wrong things. There is just no point in being pleased with ourselves for doing what it is our duty to do!

In fact I should have been ashamed at allowing myself to get over weight rather than proud at shedding it!

Too often we look for praise and thanks for doing what is our duty. A lot of "votes of thanks" should never take place for that reason!

Jesus had something to say about this: "When you have done all that is commanded you, say: 'We are unworthy servants; we have only done what was our duty!'"

Jesus wanted to know what cause for pride a man had if he loved the people who loved him, and if he greeted his brothers enthusiastically. That is the kind of thing anyone does. So Jesus asked, "What *more* are you doing than others?" (Matt. 5:47).

This is the really Christian question. There are a great many people who will claim: "Well, I'm as good as the next man anyhow."

But the whole point of the Christian life is that the Christian should not be as good as the next man; *he should be a great deal better than him*!

There is no point in Christianity unless it has something extra special.

Not only has the Christian the obligation to be something special. He has also the power to be something special. For he has God.

This is his real reason for pride. "Let him who boasts, boast of the Lord," said St. Paul (1 Cor. 1:31).

So it is not pride but humility that is the really Christian attitude.

It is what God has done through and in Jesus that is *our* boast.

Read St. Luke 17: 1–10.

Once there was a monk called Simon Stylites—who expressed his faith by sitting alone for a very long time on the top of a pole!

I don't think that possibility will appeal to you!

This is a way some people look at the world.
They *withdraw* from it.

Very early in the life of the Church there were those who decided they could only be Christian by withdrawing to the deserts. Later, monasteries and convents arose for that very reason.

These people prayed for the world but were anxious, so far as humanly possible, not to live in it.

Another attitude to the world is that of *indifference* to it. Here people choose to live in the world, but take no part in it.

This is what many people do! They love their own lives and their own circle, but are unconcerned, in any active way, about what is going on in the world unless it affects what they should receive!

They take their dues from the world.

They often forget they have duties to it!

Still others choose to be "*involved*" in the world, for they believe that only by involvement can vision become actuality.

The Christian does this because he knows that the Incarnation, that is the coming of God into our world in Jesus, was the great act of involvement God made for us.

We must "get involved"—for him.

Read St. John 1: 1–14.

There is, says the book of Ecclesiastes, "a time to laugh". Let's think about laughter today.

I think the laughter-makers, the comedians, exercise a wonderful ministry. I am grateful to them.

"Laughter," as Thomas Hobbes the philosopher said, "is nothing else than a sudden glory".

There is of course a right kind of laughter and a wrong kind. There is the snigger you sometimes hear over a dirty joke. There is cynical laughter which finds amusement in poking fun in a particularly shallow way at deep things.

But there is a laughter that is good. It is one of God's great gifts.

The same is true of singing.

We once spent a holiday in Wales, truly the land of song. It was in Llandudno. We went to the community hymn-singing, with the town brass band on the promenade at the bandstand on Sunday evening. There must have been far more than a thousand people there. The bandmaster was a genius at getting men and women and children to sing. "The Church's one foundation", "Onward, Christian Soldiers", "Pleasant are thy courts above" and, of course, "Guide me, O thou great Jehovah" to the immortal tune "Cwm Rhondda"—these and many another hymn sounded out in the summer evening sunlight.

There was a ministry there.

"They laugh and sing" it says of the trees, in an old anthem.

To laugh and to sing.

What good gifts!

Read Ecclesiastes 3: 1–8.

How often you have heard that said by the conductor or conductress.

Could we look at that thought in relation to the journey of life?

For in life you progress in proportion to the fare you are prepared to pay.

This is true of *knowledge*.

The price of the journey here is just (yes, that word again!) *work*.

So if the progress we make is in proportion to the fare we pay, then that fare is a large quantity of work, sheer hard work!

This is true of *friendship*.

It was said of one wealthy man: "With all his giving, he never gives himself".

Friendship means far more than getting, far more than using someone. It means self-giving.

It is a fare which has to be paid.

Willingly.

This is true of *life*.

If you are going to get much out of life, you must pay the fare.

There is a rough sort of justice in life: we get out of life what we put into it. If we live as if life owes us everything, we will get nothing. If we give to life, we shall receive.

This is true of *the Christian life*.

Jesus said that if we tried to save our lives, we would lose them, but if we threw them away unselfishly, we would find true living.

Are you prepared to pay the fare?

St. Matthew 10: 32–39.

Space travel is a mystery to me. I am just baffled by it all!

But for me the most astonishing and significant fact about space travel is this. When the scientists prepared things for the space flight which encircled the moon, they made every possible calculation; and they made their calculations on the basis that the laws which operate here on earth operate in exactly the same way a quarter of a million miles away. They assumed confidently that the scientific laws which operate here operate there too. And they were right.

Surely there *must* be a mind behind such order. Space travel proves that not just the earth, but the universe, is God's; that God is not a figment of earth-man's imagination, but that his mind and his laws are operative everywhere.

So there are two things we believe about God that have been confirmed.

God is universal.

The Psalmist was profoundly right: "Where shall I go from thy Spirit? Or whither shall I flee thy presence? ... If I take the wings of the morning and dwell in the uttermost parts of the sea, even there thy hand shall lead me, and thy right hand shall hold me" (Ps. 139: 7–10).

Jonah crossed half a world to get away from God—and found God still waiting for him.

God is God, not only of the world, but of the universe.

God is dependable

In their calculations, the scientists trusted the laws of nature, which are the laws of God, in part of the universe where no man had ever been—and the laws worked. The astronauts literally bet their lives on God—and they did not lose.

If the scientific laws of God are operative everywhere and utterly to be depended on, we can trust the laws of God's love too.

Science is therefore doing something to help us appreciate more fully how dependable God is and how universal.

We always believed it. To know it in this new way is even more helpful.

So let us end our half-year with some words of John Greenleaf Whittier:

> I know not where His islands lift
> Their fronded palms to air:
> I only know I cannot drift
> Beyond His love and care.

Read Psalm 139: 1–12.